TEACHER'S
ARTS AND CRAFTS
ALMANACK

TEACHER'S ARTS AND CRAFTS ALMANACK

Dena Guttman

Parker Publishing Company, Inc.   West Nyack, New York

© 1978, *by*

PARKER PUBLISHING COMPANY, INC.

West Nyack, N.Y.

Library of Congress Cataloging in Publication Data

Guttman, Dena
    Teacher's arts and crafts almanack.

    Includes index.
    1.   Creative activities and seat work.   2.   Holi-
days--United States.   I.   Title.
LB1537.G88   372.5   77-17793
ISBN 0-13-887984-2

Printed in the United States of America

A Word from the Author

The parade of changing seasons and significant events inscribed in old-fashioned farmers' "almanacks" continues to fascinate modern boys and girls. As their grandparents did before them, today's children respond with great enthusiasm to the changing look of the seasons, to special times, holidays, birthdays of famous people, and to the notable days and weeks that occur during the school year.

This interest can be sparked by you, the classroom teacher, with the presentation of valuable, original art projects relating to these events.

Teacher's Arts and Crafts Almanack is a unique collection of well over 100 practical ideas for use in your classroom that can, with your help, motivate students through artistic experiences to understand and enjoy these celebrations. I have purposely stressed readily available or easily obtainable materials for these projects.

Since holidays and special events are such natural motivators for art activities, you can also use the ideas for individual learning center activities. You need only provide the materials and copy the directions onto cards to be placed in the centers.

Step-by-step illustrations serve as your guide to what the finished products will look like, and you can make up "samples" beforehand to show your boys and girls, if you wish. Their own creative suggestions for changes should be welcomed, and your approach should be open ended.

This book can offer you a variety of interesting projects that will stimulate creativity for years to come. Many of the projects, such as cutting a star, can be undertaken year after year. These ideas are applicable to all grades, Kindergarten through 6, with variations and Bonus Activities offered for each month. I have set up the chapters according to the school calendar, September through June, so you can work right through the year. The completed projects can be displayed on bulletin boards, worn, hung up, given as gifts or greeting cards, or put to other uses.

Background information and dates are given for events seldom found in other activities source books. Contributions to our own culture of many national and ethnic traditions are reflected in these events.

Enjoyment can be an integral part of learning. Positive comments from children over the years have shown me that art experiences drawn from meaningful events of the year can be educational, inspirational, and fun.

Dena Guttman

Table of Contents

HIGHLIGHTS OF THE MONTH OF SEPTEMBER *(Cont.)*

HIGHLIGHTS OF THE MONTH OF NOVEMBER *(Cont.)*

HIGHLIGHTS OF THE MONTH OF JANUARY *(Cont.)*

HIGHLIGHTS OF THE MONTH OF MAY *(Cont.)*

HIGHLIGHTS OF THE MONTH OF JUNE *(Cont.)*

1

HIGHLIGHTS

of the month of

SEPTEMBER

Labor Day

Opening of School

Rosh Hashanah (Hebrew New Year)

Hebrew Sukkoth (Feast of Tabernacles)

National Anthem Day

Pilgrims Sail on Mayflower

Citizenship Day

Autumn Begins

American Indian Day

Henry Hudson Discovers Manhattan

Elias Howe Patents Sewing Machine

America's First Daily Newspaper Opens

Labor Day

America was the first country to establish a Labor Day. Workers and their products form an integral part of society. We celebrate the dignity and accomplishments of Labor by declaring a day of rest for workers. In 1894, the date was changed from May 1st to the first Monday in September. Most public schools begin their year on the following day.

"Butcher, baker, candlestick-maker,"—children can dress up a grouping of **connected paper dolls** to represent members of the work force in their various occupations.

Cutting on a fold is accomplished with practice. Fan-fold any long *rectangular* piece of *paper* (*newsprint* is easier for younger children to use, since several layers must be cut) and draw a boy or girl (half shape) on the fold. (See Figures 1-1A and 1-1B.) Be sure to leave a few points on the figure(s) connected to the opposite fold(s) so figures do not fall apart when cut and opened. The number of figures will vary with the number of folds and length of the paper.

If stiffer paper is used, the dolls will stand. They can be stapled or pasted into a standing circle. If half figures appear, they can be stapled together or cut off.

Use *cut paper* or *crayons* to dress up figures in their work clothes. Tools of the trade, when appropriate, may also be added. (See Figure 1-1C.)

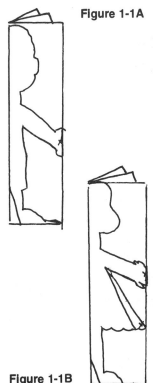

Figure 1-1A

Figure 1-1B

Figure 1-1C

Figure 1-2A

Figure 1-2B

Opening of School

An eye-catching window display called **Smile Buttons** can be created by children to welcome one another back for the new school year.

Use *black construction paper* and *yellow tissue paper* or *cellophane*. Cut two black circles (approximately the size of the bottom of a large glass). Poke scissors through both circles, and cut out eyes, nose and a mouth, all pre-drawn with a pencil or chalk. (See Figure 1-2A.)

Open up black circles in a sandwich-like fashion, spread some paste on both, insert a larger piece of tissue between, and put circles together. Trim off excess tissue. It is easier to cut if you trim away a very thin sliver of the black circle(s). (See Figure 1-2B.)

Attach to windows with small pieces of rolled (masking or clear) tape. Light will shine through these happy faces.

Younger children might make the same project using one circle only, but double-circle Smile Buttons will look better on the windows when viewed from the street.

Rosh Hashanah

Rosh Hashanah, the Jewish New Year, comes in September or

October. It is believed that God judges each person's actions during the past year, and all is recorded in the Book of Life.

Paper scrolls commemorating this holiday can be constructed from *brown butcher paper* and *two wooden dowel sticks* or *rolling pins*. (See Figure 1-3.)

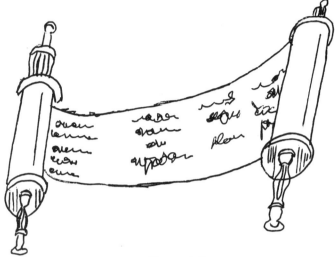

Figure 1-3

Rules of good conduct or ideas for getting along with others, formulated in classroom discussion, can be inscribed in ink on the butcher paper.

The edges of the paper can be burned slightly to give a parchment or antique quality to the scroll. This should be done carefully, under teacher supervision.

The paper is then fastened with white glue or a heavy duty stapler to the dowels or rolling pins, with which the scroll can then be unrolled from both ends.

Hebrew Sukkoth

Sukkoth, or Feast of Tabernacles, is a Hebrew harvest festival, occurring in September or October. Huts of branches, with flowers interwoven to form leafy roofs, were built in the fields to save travel time. Grain and grapes were added. Today, "sukkahs" are constructed at home or in front of temples, and are decorated with flowers, vegetables and fruits.

A **miniature sukkah** can be made from *small sticks* or *tongue* *depressors*, *glued* or put together with *small pieces* of *non-hardening clay* to form a simple frame. (See Figure 1-4A.)

Raffia and *leaves* (real or paper) can be intertwined to form a roof. *Twigs* for crosspieces can be added for a lattice-like effect. Small bunches of grapes, and other fruits and vegetables of *cut colored paper*, will add to the finished product. (See Figure 1-4B.)

Our American Thanksgiving is another harvest festival.

Figure 1-4A   Figure 1-4B

National Anthem Day

National Anthem Day is celebrated on September 14th in Maryland. "The Star Spangled Banner" was written in 1814 by Francis Scott Key, and epitomizes the spirit of patriotism in our land. It is a hymn to the flag flown from Fort McHenry during the War of 1812.

Musical mobiles (Figure 1-5A) can add spirit to any classroom.

Figure 1-5A

Use a *wire hanger* or *dowel stick*, and *thread* or *wire* to hang notes made of *black* (or *red, white* and *blue*) *construction paper*. Notes might be made of *cardboard* and painted.

By experimenting with these basic materials, several different types of mobiles may be constructed. Be sure to stress the importance of note placement so proper balance will be achieved. Hang up and enjoy!

Perhaps the music teacher can help by furnishing the actual notes for "The Star Spangled Banner." Music books will also provide this information.

As a variation for younger students, cut a circle of colored paper into a spiral and punch holes in several places. (See Figure 1-5B.)

Punch notes, and string, to hang. (See Figure 1-5C.)

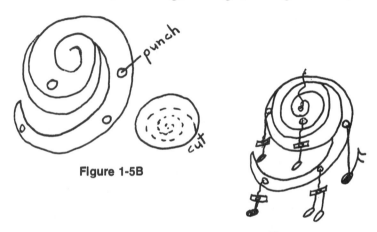

Figure 1-5B

Figure 1-5C

Pilgrims Sail on Mayflower

The Pilgrims set sail from England on the 16th of September in 1620.

One paper project, **Pilgrim Ships**, that represents this historic voyage begins with an origami boat. (See May, "National Maritime Day" illustrations.)

Paper sails, *stapled* or pushed through a *straw*, are then added.

Wavy-cut, wide *paper strips* are stapled to a background. Leave some portions of the strip standing away from the background paper for a dimensional effect. Sides (ends) of strips can be bent in twice and pasted, or stapled, for a similar look. (See Figure 1-6.)

Pieces of *purple, blue* and *green construction paper* make good color combinations for the waves.

Figure 1-6

This theme can be developed into a project called "Stormy Sea Paintings," which will require some *granulated detergent* added to *blue, green* or *purple tempera paint.* Mix, in clean *coffee cans,* to a thick, rich consistency and apply to *tagboard, cardboard* or *scrap canvas. White paint* can be used for foam or highlights on the water.

A discussion of waves, highlights, and feelings about the sea should lead to many interesting abstract action paintings. Exciting, textured (impasto) paintings can be displayed proudly.

The playing of music during this lesson might help to loosen up feelings and elicit freer, more uninhibited brush strokes.

Hopefully, paintings will be individualistic and spontaneous, so no one illustration or sample will suffice.

Citizenship Day

The United States Constitution was first adopted by a majority and signed at the Constitutional Convention in 1787. This day is also referred to as Citizenship Day. The 17th of September is celebrated annually, by Presidential proclamation, and signifies an important step towards a well-governed nation.

Pencil rubbings, using the names of some famous Americans who signed the Constitution (George Washington, Benjamin Franklin, Alexander Hamilton, James Madison) can become fascinating designs. (See Figures 1-7A and 1-7B.)

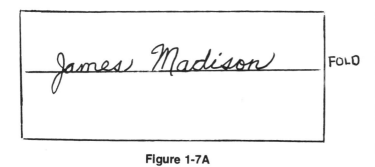

James Madison FOLD

Figure 1-7A

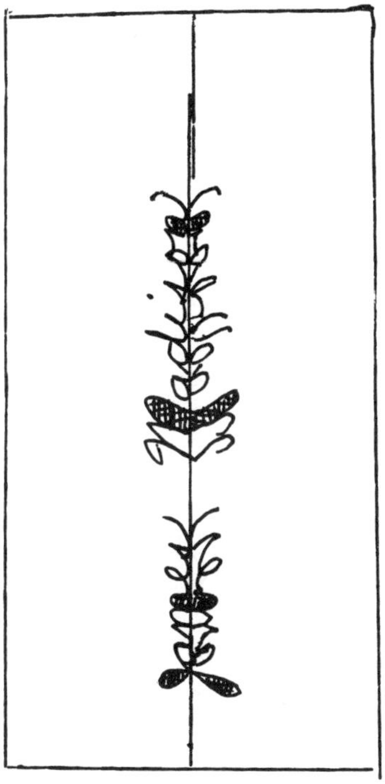

Figure 1-7B

Fold *12" x 18" white drawing paper* in half. Open. Write (cursive only) name with a *pencil* on the horizontal fold. Press hard. Re-fold and rub hard (using side of pencil lead) on the back of the paper, until the backward impression of name can be seen when paper is re-opened. Go over (re-trace) so light rubbing lines are not lost. Turn paper vertically.

Each name forms a different design. Try several. Some areas can be colored in with crayons, colored pencils or fine-line markers.

See if the children can match up names with the designs when finished.

Autumn Begins

The autumnal equinox occurs September 22nd or 23rd. This is the time when the sun crosses the equator, and night and day are of equal length in all parts of the earth.

The making of **leaf prints** is a fitting project for the beginning of the fall season.

Have the children gather interesting leaves in varying sizes and shapes. Soft leaves make better prints than brittle ones.

Thin *black* or *blue* (or other) *acrylic paints* with water, and apply evenly with *bristle* or *small acrylic brush* to underside of leaf, carefully covering veins, stem and edges. *Water-soluble block printing ink* or *thinned tempera paint* may also be tried.

Place leaf, underside down, on paper to be printed, and cover with a *paper towel*. Rub lightly, and lift. The clean-up process is simplified if printing is done on fresh *newspaper* each time.

Tissue paper makes an attractive gift wrap, with an "all over" design, and *white bond paper* becomes beautiful stationery.

Try making prints of small plants, ferns and seed pods. (See Figure 1-8.)

Figure 1-8

American Indian Day

American Indian Day falls on the fourth Friday in September. On this holiday, we honor the first Americans and the nobility of their traditions.

To commemorate this day, one school-time activity might be the creation of **paper-bag fringed vests.**

A *standard size grocery bag* can easily be obtained for each child.

With the closed end up, cut and slit according to the diagram. (See Figure 1-9A.) Cut and fringe the bottom of the bag at the open end. *Leather lacing* through punched holes, or *string,* may be added.

Figure 1-9A

Figure 1-9B

Decorate with *crayons* or *paint*, employing Indian motifs and symbols: animals, hunting or campfires scenes, etc. (See Figure 1-9B.)

The vests can be worn at a dramatization of an Indian ceremonial. Children can find records, books and plays about Indians at the library or resource center.

Children of today read about a time when Indians used shells for money. A **wampum belt** can take the children on a trip back to those days. (See Figure 1-10.)

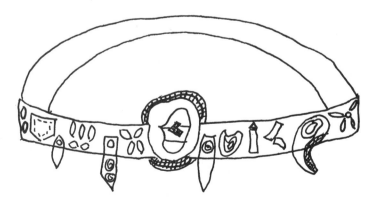

Figure 1-10

Using simple strips of *felt* and *small shells* saved from summer beach-combing, create original designs.

White glue will hold the shells in place.

An old *belt buckle* can be sewn on at the proper waist size, or a bleached, clean *marrow bone* can serve as a clasp.

For further decoration, felt pockets can be added (either sewn or glued), along with *watermelon, pumpkin* or *cantaloupe seeds*. Seeds can be pierced with a needle, or glued. They can also be dyed with vegetable dye.

Bracelets of shells and seeds, using *elastic thread*, can be made too.

Bonus Activities for September

Henry Hudson Discovers Manhattan

Henry Hudson discovered the Island of Manhattan on September 4th in 1609. This daring Englishman, employed by a company of Dutch merchants, sailed the *Half Moon* to the place we now call New York City.

Even children who have not visited this exciting city have probably seen films or pictures of its bold, twinkling skyline.

Cityscapes, an interesting experiment in painting, can result from having children imagine or envision tall, towering buildings lit up at night. (See Figure 1-11.)

Figure 1-11

Using dark colors (*tempera* or *acrylics*), and building upon a series of varying sized rectangles and other geometric shapes, add lighting effects with *yellow* and *white paint*. Of course, colored lights, billboards, traffic lights, tall radio towers, and highlighted spots from car headlights can add great interest to these paintings. Discuss the use of clusters of lights to avoid monotony.

Some may prefer to paint twilight or daytime city scenes.

Elias Howe Patents Sewing Machine

On the 10th of September, 1846, Elias Howe patented the sewing machine.

Investigations into the creation of this invention, now well known to most children, can lead to an art activity called **Paper Clothes**.

On *heavy brown paper*, design and paint the outfit of choice. Be sure to look at real clothing carefully, and discuss proper shaping, fit, etc., before beginning. Paint or color, and trim with real *buttons* and *fabric* scraps.

For a dimensional effect, cut two patterns, stuff lightly with scrap paper or newspaper, and staple.

Use a real *clothesline* and *clothespins* to display these creations when completed. (See Figure 1-12.)

Potential designers may come to the fore!

Figure 1-12

America's First Daily Newspaper Opens

On the 21st of September, 1735, America's first daily newspaper was established. John Peter Zenger published the *New York Weekly Journal*.

Living as they do in a world filled with newspapers, including school versions, children can easily identify with this form of communication, and can enjoy using it for **Newspaper Art**.

Newspaper itself is inexpensive and readily available for use as an art medium.

The classified ads, particularly, lend interest to city scenes.

Use a "look out the window" approach, or take a walk through the neighborhood, and then have the children design their own cityscape. (See Figure 1-13.)

Figure 1-13

Columns of newsprint can easily be torn on the vertical lines, or cut with scissors. Geometric shapes become realistic or domed, futuristic buildings. *Black construction paper* makes a good background for a long mural or individual pictures. Sun or moon, cars, people or pets, also of newspaper, can be added.

Some children might try using the colored comic sections from Sunday supplements.

Draw windows, store signs, doors, etc., directly on the newspaper buildings with *black markers*.

Add *gray, white* and *black construction paper* to your supply of newspaper, and you have the makings for **posters** to stimulate and advertise reading!

The librarian will love to display some of them, and so would any special teachers of reading, so share your posters with the rest of the school!

Emphasize the characteristics of good poster and advertisement design. Discussion of free-form lettering, comic "balloons" containing a few words, and simple desks, chairs, tables, and figures of people reading will stimulate the young artist toward successful results. For an example, see Figure 1-14.

Figure 1-14

2

HIGHLIGHTS
of the month of
OCTOBER

Launching of *Sputnik*

Child Health Day

Fire Prevention Week

Columbus Day

United Nations Day

American Education Week

Veterans' Day

Halloween

Poetry Day

Noah Webster's Birthday

United States Day

Navy Day

Launching of *Sputnik*

On the 4th of October, in 1957, *Sputnik*, the first artificial satellite, was launched by the Russians. This heralded the beginning of space exploration, which seems so familiar now.

Collect *boxes* of different sizes. Cover with *aluminum foil* and other *shiny* or *adhesive papers*.

Moon Men (Figure 2-1A) can come to life with a little ingenuity. *Staples* and strong *glue* are used to attach the parts. Experiment and rearrange before attaching.

Figure 2-1A

The "men" can be covered with papier mâché or plaster-craft strips and painted, for a different approach.

Pipe cleaners and all sorts of *"found"* *materials* may be employed in these robot-like constructions.

Moon Men make imaginative toys which the students can keep or give to younger sisters and brothers.

These figures can also be part of planetary travel scenes.

If cardboard boxes are not available, boxes made of *sturdy paper* will also work well for this project.

Fold a square into thirds, both ways. Cut as in Figure 2-1B.

Boxes will be open on one end after folding up. Make in several sizes. Paste together and add foil to open sections where visible.

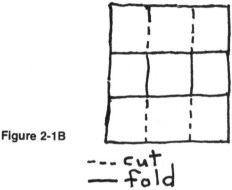

Figure 2-1B

--- cut
— fold

Child Health Day

The first Monday in October is Child Health Day by Presidential proclamation. The first observance was in 1928. In 1959, Congress changed the date from May 1st.

Proper food is vital to the health of both children and adults.

Realistic foods (see Figure 2-2), drawn with *oil crayons*, can become part of nutrition charts.

Figure 2-2

Actual foods can be used as models, or children can draw from memory. The former is a valuable lesson in still-life drawing with attention to detail.

Since oil crayons are blendable, results will look "good enough to eat"!

An array of tempting popular foods, such as hot dogs, pizza, ice cream, etc., can be displayed next to an exhibit of fruits and vegetables. The nutritional merits of each can then be compared and discussed.

Exercise, as well as proper eating habits, relates to Child Health Day.

Movable action figures (see Figure 2-3) are constructed of *paper* geometric *shapes* (oval, trapezoid, circle, rectangle, etc.). Cut two arms, two legs, two hands, at the same time by stacking the papers.

Attach with *brads* (paper fasteners) so movement of the body parts can be accomplished.

Figures can be "dressed" in *paper* clothes, cut-out clothes from *magazines*, or colored with *crayons*.

They can be placed in scenes representing various athletic activities, such as baseball, basketball, bicycling, running, jumping rope, etc.

The creation of these figures is a painless way to introduce children to some of the anatomical insights necessary for good drawing: the head is approximately one ninth of the body; certain parts of the body flex and bend; etc.

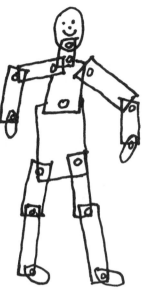

Figure 2-3

Fire Prevention Week

Fire Prevention Week always begins on the 9th, which is the anniversary of the Great Chicago Fire, October 9–11, in 1871. 17,000 buildings burned down during this time, and losses amounted to $200 million.

Mrs. O'Leary's cow kicked over a lantern in a barn on DeKoven Street, and started the fire that destroyed a large part of the city.

For a **spin art fireplace,** fold a *3½" x 5" unlined white index card* in half. A *5" x 8"* card or stiff paper can be used for a larger version of spin art.

Open card after folding. In the middle of top half, draw and color a fire. In the middle of bottom section, draw and color a fireplace. (See Figure 2-4.)

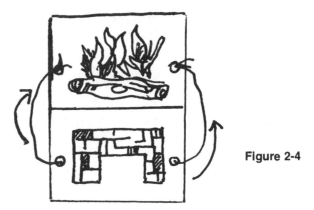

Figure 2-4

Punch holes. Attach and tie a short piece of *string* to both sides, with card in folded position. Card may be pasted together, first.

Using both hands, twirl card so string winds up, and pull firmly. Fire will appear to be inside the fireplace!

Further tries can include bird in a birdcage, fish in a fishbowl, bird in a tree, etc. Fun for all!

Columbus Day

Columbus Day is celebrated annually on the second Monday in October, by Presidential proclamation.

In 1492, Columbus landed on San Salvador, imagined he had discovered a new way to India, and opened the New World to discovery. We now know that he was not the first man to see the Western Hemisphere, but the settlement and building up of our land stemmed from his voyages.

Ship in a bottle (Figure 2-5) is made from *acetate plastic* pieces (5″ x 9″ size is adequate). Cut two bottles by using a simple pattern or drawing directly on the acetate.

Figure 2-5

Gummed colored tape or *construction paper* ship and water shapes are placed on one bottle. Overlay on the other, and staple together. Add a *brown paper* "cork."

If acetate sheets are not obtainable, make the bottle from paper, and cover with see-through *plastic wrap*.

For a **balloon globe**, which can be another project inspired by the story of Columbus, cover a large, round blown-up *balloon* with any papier mâché recipe, such as newspaper strips soaked in wheat or wallpaper paste, or prepared plastercraft strips.

Allow to dry. When using papier mâché, a final layer of paper towel strips may be added for a better painting surface. Draw the continents in pencil and fill in with paint. The remainder of the globe can be painted blue to resemble water. Use *tempera paint*.

Columbus' voyages may be traced with *marker* or paint. A "key" can be added.

Cut paper shapes of the continents can be applied, instead of paint, in decoupage fashion. Use an *acrylic medium* or *varnish*.

Finished globes can be put on stands of wood or triangularly folded heavy paper, or suspended in mobile-like fashion by the addition of a *screw* (with an eye) and *string* or *wire*.

A **tissue paper mosaic floral** is both attractive and eye-catching, and can be used to illustrate the fact that Columbus landed in a semi-tropical part of the Western Hemisphere.

Sketch (with a pencil) a flower or floral outline on *construction paper*. Tear and apply tissue shapes, overlapping. Color upon color produces dramatic blends and changes the results. Use *tissue collage glue* or *acrylic polymer gloss medium*. Both act as adhesives and create shine. *White glue*, thinned with water, may be used as a substitute.

When dry, cut out and mount on *12" x 18" white construction paper*.

Tissue collage can also be done directly on a sheet of *acetate*. Tear and apply in the same way, creating a flower. Background can be shades of *green tissue*.

Mount (staple) the result, acetate side up, on a section of *white mat board* for a frame.

Both methods produce a bright, stained glass mosaic effect.

Bonus: Any lively piece of recorded Spanish music can serve as an integral part of an unusual painting lesson.

Some children can work at easels; others on their desks. "Paint" with pieces of *white candles* in rhythm to the music, on

Figure 2-6

white paper. Designs become visible when painted over with *water colors* or *thinned tempera*.

The candle wax "resists" the paint, as in crayon-resist pictures. This project is even more exciting, however, because the white candle wax design does not appear until the paint is applied!

For **stained glass tissue windows** (reminiscent of those Columbus might have seen in Portugal and Spain), cut a leaded look design, rectangular or domed, on the fold of *12" x 18"* (or larger) *black construction paper*. (See Figure 2-6.) Open. Apply assorted colors of *tissue paper* on the back, pasting on the thick black lines that simulate the leading.

If they are to be used as window decorations, cut the "windows" *double*, open like a sandwich, and paste the tissue "filling" on the bottom window first. Then apply paste to black lines of the second window, overlay, and close the sandwich.

Daylight shines through the transparent tissue, creating exciting windows that will elicit compliments!

United Nations Day

United Nations Day is October 24th. The United Nations began in 1945 at San Francisco through a series of conferences, and has had its headquarters in New York City since 1946. It is an international organization of nations pledged to promote security and peace in the world. Nations seek to observe international law and further social progress.

In an activity you might call **Flags Around the World**, have children create their own flags or reproduce flags of the world with *glue* (mucilage or white) and *string*.

On a piece of *tagboard* or *cardboard*, lightly sketch a flag. For stripes and stars, etc., outline with glue and adhere string to the glue. Glue designs, without string, will be raised and can be printed. Let dry.

Be sure to have children write their names in pencil if lesson is to be continued at another time.

Using *water*- (or oil-) *based printing inks*, roll on with a *brayer* and print several.

Experiment with different size prints, *assorted color papers, tissue,* etc. Then have children choose their most successful print for a bulletin board display.

An activity on **paper cylinder dolls** (Figure 2-7), representing the countries of the world, would benefit from some preparatory research on national costumes.

Figure 2-7

The dolls are made from a cylinder of *12" x 18" white construction paper*. (See April: "Cylinder Clowns.")

Employ basic shapes: oval for head, rectangular strips for arms and legs. Add *fringed cut paper,* or *wool* or *string* for hair.

Wherever possible, cut two hands, two feet, etc., at the same time.

Additions, such as a piece of *fabric* for a serape, etc., will add a realistic touch to the character.

Stand the dolls on a table or window ledge and admire!

American Education Week

American Education Week is usually the last week in October—the 26th through November 1st. The date varies, but since 1970 it has been issued annually by Presidential proclamation.

Its purpose is to serve as a concentrated effort to let the public know what is happening in the schools. Exhibits are prepared and visitation days are held.

Make **classroom dioramas,** or small scenes, and put them on view for parents and friends to enjoy.

Fold *any color 12" x 18" construction paper* into thirds, the short way. Fold back the last flap. Tape together (with *masking tape*) so side view(s) is a triangle. (See Figure 2-8A.)

Turn, so that taped side is in back.

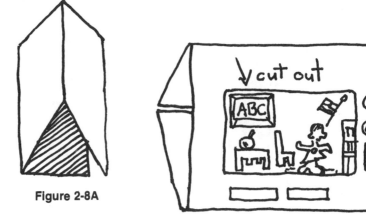

Figure 2-8A

Figure 2-8B

Poking with scissors, cut an oval or rectangangle from the front section.

Inside, set up small cut paper figures showing various classroom activities. Insert a background sheet, colored to represent your classroom.

Make paper figures with an extra tab at the bottom for folding and pasting so they stand. (See Figure 2-8B.)

The outside of the diorama can be decorated or labeled, as you wish.

These dimensional scenes would be points of interest if displayed on each child's desk for Parents' Night.

A project called **Paper Classmates** can be done in a realistic or modern way.

Work with very large pieces of *heavy brown mural paper*, on classroom floor or in the hall. Children lie down flat on the paper, and trace around each other, working in pairs. Arms should be outstretched.

Decorate with a heavy application of *crayon*, or *paint*.

Try for a likeness by paying attention to features, clothing worn that day, and other identifying characteristics, such as glasses, hair ribbons, etc. A full-length mirror would be helpful for self-observation.

Cut out these giant likenesses and tape (with clear tape) to each child's chair, in a seated position. Tape hands to desk.

It's fun to see if parents can find their "child" when they visit.

For a modern approach, paint or crayon figure(s) with

psychedelic designs and mount on the wall or in the hall outside the classroom. Fluorescent paint could make these paper people "glow"!

Another project is a **school made of cardboard.**

Have children investigate the architectural background of your school plant, whether new or old. Study interesting details firsthand. A talk by any administrator connected with buildings would be helpful.

Small models (*boxes*) or large models (*cartons*) can be attempted. Rolls of *plaster-impregnated material* are readily available. Cut into strips and dipped in water, these pieces can cover and join boxes to resemble any structure.

Drying time is much shorter than when papier mâché is used, and fewer covering layers are required.

Buildings can then be painted. Windows and doors should be cut out beforehand. Knives or razor-like tools should be used under teacher supervision.

Additional details, like a chimney, can be made of *cardboard* or *rolled newspaper*, also covered with the same material.

Smaller models can be displayed on a large table.

Futuristic visions of school buildings can be attempted.

Halloween

October 31st is Halloween, or All Hallow's Eve. It is an ancient celebration that combines the Druid autumn festival with Christian customs. The wearing of costumes is a custom emanating from pre-Christian England, when disguises were worn to confuse the spirits.

Other countries celebrate according to their own unique customs and superstitions.

Directions for an origami airplane can be found in the December chapter under "Wright Brothers Day." Now we find that the plane can be transformed into a **scary witch!** (See Figure 2-9.)

Make it from *9" x 12" black lightweight poster paper* or *12" x 18" construction paper* for a larger version.

Hold with the point at the top. Paste a *white* oval, decorated with black cut paper or crayon face, far enough down from the top so that the point becomes the hat.

Add a black strip, with hands cut from it, for arms. Attach

Figure 2-9

straggly black fringed paper for hair. Add an *orange* cut paper skirt and broom.

If necessary, cut the bottom of the plane so that the witch stands, or paste to a background, if you prefer.

Strip and fastener pumpkins require ten nine-inch long, *orange construction paper strips*. Stack them. Push a paper fastener through one end, one or two strips at a time. Repeat this procedure at the other end of the strips, using a second fastener. Be sure strips are at least one inch wide. (See Figure 2-10A.)

Spread apart evenly, creating a rounded "pumpkin" shape.

Decorate with ears, eyes, nose, mouth and hair of cut *black paper*. Staple or paste on. (See Figure 2-10B.)

Attach a piece of *orange* or *black wool* to top fastener to facilitate carrying or hanging.

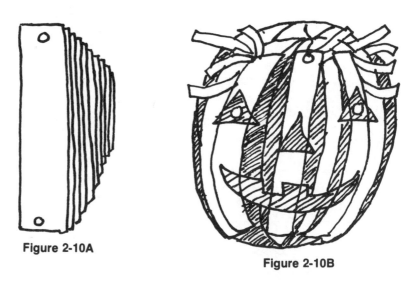

Figure 2-10A

Figure 2-10B

Bonus Activities for October

Poetry Day

October 15th is Poetry Day. October 7th is Black Poetry Day. The list of great poets is long, from Jupiter Hammon, first black in America to publish his own verse, to the Brownings, Emerson,

Frost, Keats, Stevenson, Whitman, and others far too numerous to list. All were born during the school year. Familiarity with their work is both exciting and important to children.

Allow children to explore the world of poetry through exposure to readings, records and books of verse, and through informal discussion.

Original, spontaneous poetry writing should be encouraged throughout the school year.

In the upper grades, favorite stanzas or portions can be incorporated into **picture poems** depicting selected parts of the poem.

In the lower grades, picture poems can be illustrated with one word, written around an animal or figure, taken from a favorite poem. Examples could include a horse, elephant, etc.

The words are intertwined, or interlaced into the picture, wherever feasible.

For example, Robert Frost's ''Stopping by Woods on a Snowy Evening'' might be illustrated in any medium. *Pen* and *ink* renditions of picture poems would be effective. If a woodland scene is drawn, the words can ''amble'' in and about the tree branches, or around a horse and rider. (See Figure 2-11.)

Some children might want to do several, creating a notebook or a series of drawings on a favorite poet.

Figure 2-11

Noah Webster's Birthday

Noah Webster, 1758–1843, was the American lexicographer who compiled *Webster's Dictionary* in 1828. His birthday is the 16th of October.

The idea of dictionaries can inspire a **crossword puzzle design project.** Study crossword puzzles clipped from newspapers, magazines and school publications.

Older children can utilize dictionaries in making original puzzles.

Perhaps some of the puzzles can have a theme that centers around classroom activities, or names of classmates.

A June chapter activity entitled ''Modern Hieroglyphic Design'' uses an approach allied to the concept of interlocking.

Rulers and *crayons* can be used in making designs related to the crossword puzzle. (See Figure 2-12.)

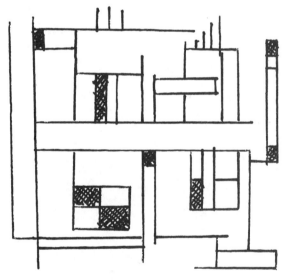

Figure 2-12

Geometric or cubistic painting might be a further outgrowth of these lessons.

United States Day

United States Day is October 23rd. Its sponsor is the United

States Day Committee, Inc., of Tulsa, Oklahoma. The purpose is "to maintain the U.S. as a sovereign, independent nation under the Constitution, without limitation by treaty or supergovernment."

State puzzles can be traced from a map or drawn freehand on paper. Begin with your own state, and continue with others.

Cut out and paste on *light cardboard*. Label cities, etc., coloring as you wish. Cut apart into puzzle-like shapes that will fit together. (See Figure 2-13.)

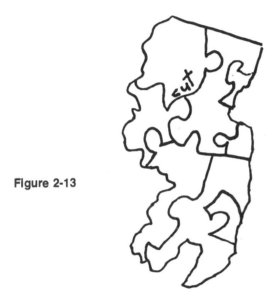

Figure 2-13

Be sure pieces are not too small, and that they can interlock.

A puzzle map of the whole country could be done in wood and cut out with a jigsaw, if individual states are made to scale.

Navy Day

Navy Day, October 27, has been observed since 1922. Children are interested in this branch of the Armed Services connected with the seas and sailing.

The origami boat (see May chapter) doubles as a **sailor hat**, if made in a larger size.

For more fun, have children pretend the sailor has been shipwrecked and saved, leaving his shirt behind!

Tear the boat in three places (See Figure 2-14.)

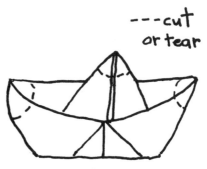

Figure 2-14

Open it up. You have found his shirt!

If the boat/hat is made from a large sheet of newspaper, children can color and wear the shirt.

3

HIGHLIGHTS
of the month of
NOVEMBER

Election Day
Bird Migrations Begin
Robert Fulton's Birthday
National Children's Book Week
Puerto Rican Discovery Day
Latin American Day
Thanksgiving
Sojourner Truth Day
Youth Appreciation Week
Mayflower Compact Day
Birthday of the Author of *Pinocchio*

Election Day

Election Day is the first Tuesday after the first Monday in November. The election for President of the United States is held every four years, and for Representatives, every two years. Voting is both a right and a privilege, and one of the strengths of our form of government. Election Day was set by an Act of Congress in 1854, and is a legal holiday in most states.

A three-dimensional project called **City Scenes** can easily depict a police station, fire house, or other public building.

Cut *paper* rectangles and squares of varying dimensions. Fold in the two side edges of each one twice. Apply *paste* to last folded strip so the paper (building) has sides. (See Figure 3-1A.)

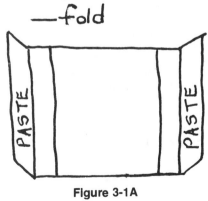

Figure 3-1A

Roll some pieces of paper into cylindrical shapes, for towers, etc.

Lettering adds to the composition. Windows and doors can be cut directly (by folding paper) or pasted on in contrasting colors (small squares).

While any color combinations can be used (red, white and blue for a patriotic theme), black, white, gray and newspaper are quite effective.

Remind children to select one color for the background, and leave it intact. Cut the others into squares, etc.

Shapes can be built up in a layered fashion by inserting one inside the other. For one possible outcome, see Figure 3-1B.

Figure 3-1B

Gather a pile of magazines or colored newspaper sections containing front view faces for **half-a-face drawings.**

Selected faces are cut in half vertically and pasted (one of the two pieces) onto one side of *white 12" x 18" drawing* or *construction paper*. With pencil, crayon or marker, etc., children will be surprised at how easily they can reproduce the other half through close observation and attention to detail. Color can be added for closer resemblance, although half of the face done in line only can also be striking.

Right-handed children usually find it easier to paste the left side of the magazine face, so they can draw on the right side. The opposite would be true for left-handed children.

Using the cut paper face as a guide, many children will be encouraged enough by their success to attempt full-face drawing on their own with less trepidation.

The results create comment when displayed.

Younger children can experience **"voting"** in a simplified manner.

Use *flash cards* or the like and color pictures of different birds or animals. *Cut paper* pictures or *magazine* pictures might also be used. Children choose their favorite one.

These simple "ballots" can be inserted into a slot in a decorated *box* or *carton*. Class-appointed election officers then count the ballots and declare the victor(s). The winning bird or animal might be used as a class emblem or insignia.

Reading groups, teams, etc., can use these symbols too.

A campaign, with speeches and posters, can be waged before the voting takes place.

Elections for class officers can be carried on in a similar manner. Pictures of the candidates can be drawn, or photographs taken by older children, for an interesting variation that employs yet another art technique.

Ballots can be printed by the children, or reproduced in several ways.

Bird Migration Begins

Bird migrations begin in November. Birds then move from one region to another with the change of seasons. Some travel alone; others in flocks.

Scientists say the varying amount and intensity of sunlight on birds at certain times creates the urge to travel.

The four main flyways in North America that birds use as skyways are the Atlantic, Mississippi, Central and Pacific.

To make a **paper sculpture bird**, fold a *sheet* (any color desired) of *12" x 18" construction paper* in half, lengthwise. On the fold, draw or trace the stylized bird shown in Figure 3-2A.

Cut out and score on the solid lines; fold on the broken lines. (See Figure 3-2B.)

These lines can be drawn on lightly in pencil first.

To assemble, press gently on scored lines. Tail pops up, and the fold goes down. Beak can be stapled. This bird can be a stabile or a mobile.

Decorate with crayon beforehand, or afterward with cut paper feathers or imaginative designs.

Try smaller sizes, also.

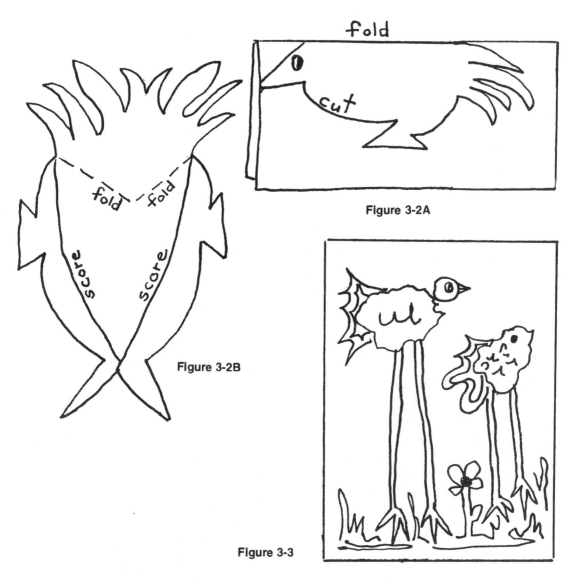

Figure 3-2A

Figure 3-2B

Figure 3-3

Torn paper and crayon birds are fun for younger children.
Have them tear an oval shape from any color *poster paper* or
construction paper. This shape becomes the bird's body. Paste onto
a contrasting background. With *crayon*, add fanciful feathers, long
legs, head and beak, etc. Some children will continue their pictures,
adding grass and flowers, and crayoned simulated feathers directly
onto the torn shape. This mixed media project results in unusual,
somewhat surrealistic birds, instead of realistic representations.
(See Figure 3-3.)

Veterans' Day

Veterans' Day which falls on November 11th, is a legal public holiday.

Also known as Armistice Day, it celebrates the anniversary of the Armistice between Allied and Central Powers, signed in 1918 in France.

An activity on **poster lettering** shows that clear lettering enhances any poster, patriotic or not. There are many ways to cut block capital letters. When children gain confidence in cutting letters that are uniform, they can attempt free-form and fancy cutting.

For practice, cut up rectangles 1½" x 2" (or larger) from *newsprint*. Students can begin with their first name.

A dittoed direction sheet(s) for each child would be helpful. It

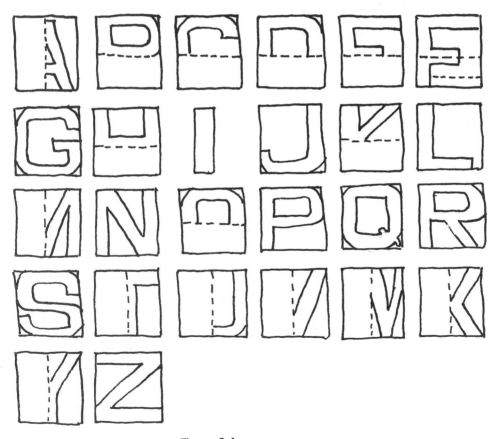

Figure 3-4

could be inserted into a notebook or folder and kept for future reference.

Directions for this method are simple: fold on dotted lines; cut on solid. Some letters are cut from the rectangle without folding. (See Figure 3-4.)

Cut letters for posters from desired colors of *construction paper* and add other elements. *Red, white, blue* and *silver* are the obvious colors for a patriotic theme; others may be used.

Children will find their letter-cutting skills very useful for many other art projects.

Robert Fulton's Birthday

Robert Fulton, an American inventor known for the steamboat, was born November 14, 1765, and died February 24, 1815. Actually, he built the *Clermont* in 1807 by studying and following the plans of John Fitch. On September 4, 1807, the *Clermont's* engines moved the ship up the Hudson River to Albany.

To make replicas of **the Clermont**, *paper towel cardboard rolls* with *cotton* for "steam" can be stapled into cardboard boats. The basic boat can be a long, somewhat canoe-like shape. Bend and

Figure 3-5

staple two of these shapes to stand, and add sails of *paper* or *white tissue paper*. A flag and a cardboard paddlewheel can be added. Folded paper (box shapes) can serve as decks, and string added to the sails. Use of basic reference pictures can serve as inspiration. Older children can take this project quite far. Boats can be painted, if desired. (See Figure 3-5.)

National Children's Book Week

National Children's Book Week (November 17–23) is sponsored by the Children's Book Council, Inc., of New York City. Librarians, teachers and parents can cooperate all year round by exposing children to literature, and fostering a love for reading that can bring life-long fulfillment.

Familiarity with the alphabet can be accomplished and strengthened through art. Young children will enjoy constructing **flash cards**. Cut up *stiff paper* into any size that can be easily handled. On each card, draw one large capital letter. Markers make a bold image and children enjoy using them.

Use crayons to change each letter into a cartoon figure, animal, etc. Demonstrate the simplicity of adding lines for feet and arms to an "A," or creating a face inside the top section of a "B." The possibilities are unlimited. (See Figure 3-6.)

Figure 3-6

If one color only is used for the letters, they will remain visible even after the cartooning is done.

Make up letter recognition games.

Children can continue, working in their spare time at their own pace, until all 26 letters are completed.

Numbers can also be done in the same way.

Besides combining art and reading, this project is good for an individualized learning center activity.

Blot painting book covers jacket any book handsomely.

Use any *sturdy paper*, but be sure it is quite a bit larger than the book. Fold in half. Open. Drip or squirt *black ink* or *tempera paint* in any color on the fold. Thin paint first with water. Re-fold, press lightly, and open. Results will vary.

Patterns and designs can be left as is or elaborated upon with ink or brush. Details may be added to "blots" so that figures, etc., emerge. When dry, fold to fit book. Fold top and bottom edges in to match the size of the book. Lay book on top. Fold in sides so pocket flaps for back and front covers are created. Then slip in covers of book. (See Figures 3-7A and 3-7B.)

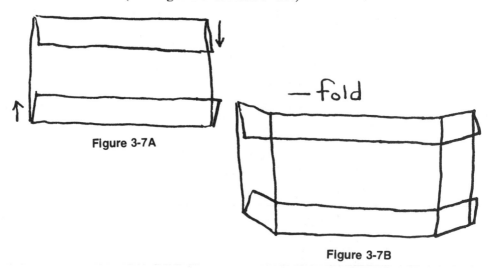

Figure 3-7A

Figure 3-7B

Felt and glue hand puppets, made from a basic outline shape, can become favorite story folk.

Cut two identical *felt* shapes. (See Figure 3-8A.) Open; glue edges all around with *white glue*. Be sure to leave the bottom open so hand can be inserted.

A sewn, overhand stitch all around the puppet might be substituted, if preferred.

Figure 3-8A

Decorate with contrasting colored felt scraps. Save pieces left over from cutting the basic shape(s) for students to share. Raffia, cotton or wool may be used for hair. Real buttons or other trimmings add to the originality and uniqueness of individual puppets. (See Figure 3-8B.)

Figure 3-8B

Dialogues can be written or stories acted out. A simple puppet stage may be constructed, or youngsters can kneel behind a high table to put on their "show."

Puerto Rican Discovery Day

Puerto Rican Discovery Day is November 19. Celebrations are held honoring Columbus' discovery of Puerto Rico in 1493. It was on his second trip that he landed with some men to establish farms and towns. Some gold and pearls were found, but no rich cities.

The **map of Puerto Rico** is a relatively simple shape to reproduce. Trace, or draw on *12" x 18" paper*, and cut out by poking scissors through the paper. Overlay on a *contrasting color paper* and label the areas in ink. (See Figure 3-9.)

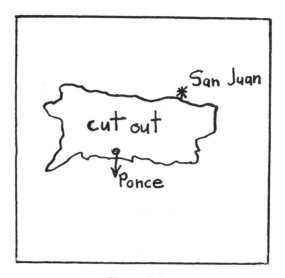

Figure 3-9

Acetate or *tissue* overlays can also be employed, detailing products, topography, etc.

Perhaps children from these places can contribute first-hand background information.

A copy of the **Puerto Rican flag** can be reproduced from *red, white* and *blue felt*. (See Figure 3-10.)

Felt pieces can be glued or sewn. A narrow strip at left edge of the flag can be sewn or stapled onto a *dowel stick* for use in class or auditorium pageants or display purposes.

The **piñata,** usually a form made of clay or papier mâché containing toys and candy, is hung from the ceiling on certain festivals. It is then broken with a stick.

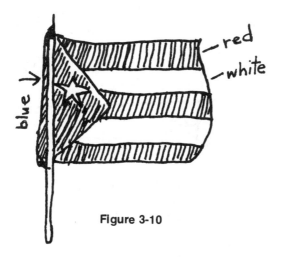

Figure 3-10

A plain brown *paper bag*, stuffed with small goodies, can serve as well. Tie with an elastic band. Cover with brightly colored, fringed *tissue paper*. Curl fringes with scissors, and staple on or paste in layers. Smaller bags can be stuffed with newspaper and added on to create head and legs of a decorative animal.

Tie a string around the piñata(s) and suspend. Hit with a stick to release the surprises. If children are blindfolded, be careful! Use to celebrate Puerto Rican Discovery Day. (See Figure 3-11.)

Figure 3-11

Use *colored paper* to cut a **still life** showing the important foods of Puerto Rico. Bananas, coconuts, coffee, pineapples and plantains are some of them. Other cut paper scenes can include sugar cane, rice, hogs and beef cattle. Some children might create interesting repetitive patterns using just one product like the pineapple. (See Figure 3-12.)

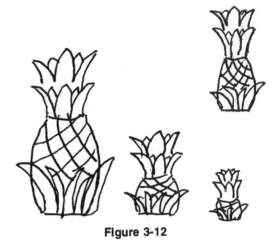

Figure 3-12

The **seal of Puerto Rico**, found in several reference books, utilizes the lamb as a symbol of peace and brotherhood. Oil crayons, fine-line markers, or other media can be used to reproduce the seal for large posters.

Application of cotton can make the lamb "woolly." Portions of the seal can be attempted by some and assembled in a group effort. (See Figure 3-13.)

Figure 3-13

Latin America Day

Latin America Day is the day before Thanksgiving. Latin America Week is November 23–29. Its purpose is to promote closer economic and cultural ties with all Latin republics and the United States on the community level.

To capture the light and excitement of a festive atmosphere, have the class make an **abstract movie.**

Several graphic art supply houses handle *acetate film*; specifically, *clear, double-perforated* (for silent) *16mm, leader*. Old film can also be bleached, but takes time and effort.

100-foot rolls run for approximately 2¼ minutes. Film can be ordered in 200- or 250-foot rolls, etc., if longer ones are desired. Cost is minimal. Keep in mind that 100-foot rolls take a long time to finish.

Children simply draw, doodle or scribble on the film with overhead projection markers that are easily obtainable.

Put two or three long tables together. Lay out the blank film and secure ends with masking tape. As the film is worked on, lift tape, roll, and move film down until remainder of the roll is completed. Attach film to a projection reel, and show.

Immediate viewing is dramatic, because frames are projected at 24 per second.

Any combination of colors, scribbles, or even written words produces unanticipated, lively and interesting results. Accompany with appropriate music on a phonograph or use tape cassettes.

If other films are attempted, children can begin to control results to a greater degree by repetition of several frames.

The class-produced films generate excitement for an assembly program, meeting, etc.

Thanksgiving

Thanksgiving Day is celebrated in November by Presidential proclamation issued annually for the fourth Thursday. It is a legal public holiday and observed in all the states. George Washington proclaimed the first national Thanksgiving on the 26th in 1789.

We usually celebrate with a feast of turkey and the trimmings like the Thanksgiving dinner enjoyed by the Indians and Pilgrim Fathers of Governor Bradford's Plymouth Colony.

One enjoyable activity, combining origami, cut paper and drawing, is the making of a **Pilgrim head.**

To make the hat, fold paper to obtain a paper cup. Start with a square of *white paper, 8" x 8"* or larger. With any point on the square on top, fold into a triangle (Figure 3-14A).

Fold left bottom edge over to right side, keeping top fold straight (Figure 3-14B).

Fold right bottom edge over to left side in the same way (Figure 3-14C.)

Fold top flaps down on both sides to finish the cup (Figure 3-14D.)

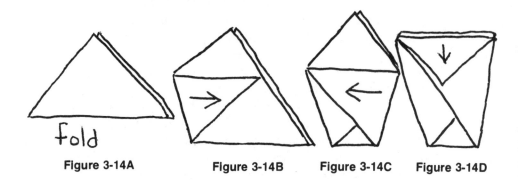

| Figure 3-14A | Figure 3-14B | Figure 3-14C | Figure 3-14D |

Invert, and cup becomes a hat for a Pilgrim.

Cut face, collar and hair in simple geometric shapes (oval, rectangle, circle) (Figure 3-14E). Use dark colors (black, brown, gray). Add features of cut paper or crayon, ink, paint or marker. These can be mounted on contrasting colored construction paper or displayed unmounted.

| Figure 3-14E | Figure 3-14F |

Braided yellow paper or raffia creates "pigtails" for a Pilgrim girl. (See Figure 3-14F.)

For another lesson, simple-shape bodies may be added.

Multiple turkeys of *brown, white, black* and *gray 12" x 18" paper* are unusual. Cut three identical outline shapes of a simple turkey. Save one color of your choice for the background. The turkey shape should be drawn lightly in pencil first, after referring to pictures.

After cutting, save all the "negative" shape turkey papers.

Paste (overlap) the three "positive" turkeys so that all the colors show. (See Figure 3-15A.)

Figure 3-15A

For a second picture, mount the negative papers in a similar way (turkeys slightly askew) so some of each color shows. (See Figure 3-15B.)

Figure 3-15B

Turkeys can also be done smaller, on 9″ x 12″ paper, but larger ones are more effective.

Sojourner Truth Day

Sojourner Truth Day is November 26. She was an American abolitionist, civil rights leader and lecturer. Born a slave named Isabella, freed in New York in 1827, she became an eloquent black feminist who lectured for women's rights. She died in Michigan in 1883.

Chalk in different colors works well in **stenciling**.

Sojourner Truth's name and/or silhouette can be used for this activity.

For the name, draw large block letters on 12″ x 18″ or larger paper, and cut out (poke scissors) carefully. This is the negative stencil. Save the letters.

Overlay onto another paper, outline letters inside with chalk, and, using finger or a tissue, rub inward, all around each letter. Lift stencil. (See Figure 3-16A.)

Using the individual letters saved, place on another paper, and rub outwards, away from the letter, to create the positive picture. (See Figure 16-B.) Hair spray or fixative can then be sprayed on to prevent smearing.

Figure 3-16A

Figure 3-16B

Proceed with head silhouette in the same way, creating both positive and negative results (See Figures 3-16C and 3-16D.)

Figure 3-16C

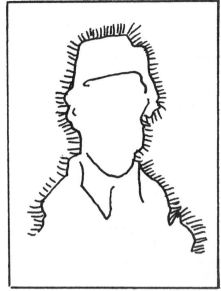

Figure 3-16D

Bonus Activities for November

Youth Appreciation Week

Figure 3-17A

Youth Appreciation Week is November 10–16. It is sponsored by Optimist International of St. Louis, Missouri. Its purpose is to recognize that most youngsters lead constructive lives in school, home and community.

Medals and lollipops can be constructed of *cardboard* and *shiny* or metallic *paper. Tinfoil* can be used as a substitute for the paper if none is available. Brightly colored *yarn* or *string* can also be applied with *white glue*.

Large cardboard lollipops could also be painted with *fluorescent paint*. If you can, use real ones readily obtainable at resort areas or speciality shops, for motivation. They come in different colors and patterns that are usually interesting swirls. (See Figures 3-17A and 3-17B.)

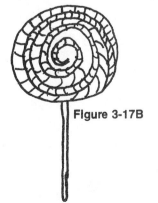

Figure 3-17B

Mayflower Compact Day

Mayflower Compact Day is November 21st. We recognize the signing of the Mayflower Compact in 1620. This document, which gave the Pilgrims the right to govern themselves, was signed in the cabin of the ship *Mayflower* before it landed in the New World.

An interesting activity which combines the New England background and the idea of writing something is the creating of attractive **notepaper**.

Any *white paper*, such as *vellum*, serves well as notepaper. Cut it to a suitable size. 7″ x 11″ folded to 3½″ x 5½″ allows ample room for drawing on the front.

The drawing should be done in *ink* or *fine-line markers* (*brown* or *black*). Have the children study professionally done notepaper, postcards and pictures of the New England area. Historic references are plentiful: lighthouses, harbor scenes, monuments, bridges. (See Figures 3-18A and 3-18B.)

Figure 3-18A

Figure 3-18B

Notepaper can be horizontal or vertical. Older students can try several styles of sketching. Some might prefer pencil sketching first.

Try to find flat boxes for the notepaper. Children can create original labels for the boxes and practice signatures during follow-up lessons.

Birthday of the Author of *Pinocchio*

Carlo Lorenzini (Collodi), born in 1826, was the Italian author of the famous story ''Pinocchio,'' which remains a classic tale, and is a favorite with many children.

In an activity inspired by the woodcarver Gepetto's creation, **Pinocchio** can be drawn, painted, or constructed of cut paper.

Draw Pinocchio's face.

Roll a cone by cutting a half-circle from a stiff piece of paper. See March chapter directions for ''Cone Bunnies.''

Make a hole in the face and insert cone nose or slash flat end of cone in several places and paste down on face. (See Figure 3-19A.)

A variation that would be fun: Pinocchio paper marionette made with (1) cut paper pieces, or (2) rolled rectangles connected with brads. Add strings to arms and legs and tie to a dowel stick or piece of wood. (See Figures 3-19B and 3-19C.)

Figure 3-19A

Figure 3-19B

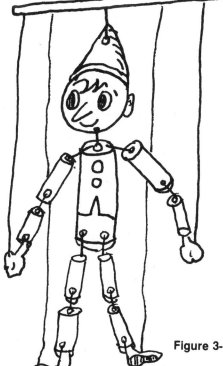

Figure 3-19C

4

HIGHLIGHTS
of the month of
DECEMBER

Festival of Lights (Chanukah)

St. Nicholas Day (European Festivals)

Human Rights Day

Wright Brothers Day (First Flight at Kitty Hawk)

Pilgrims Landed

Winter Begins

Christmas

Washington's Crossing of the Delaware

New Year's Eve

Rudyard Kipling's Birthday

Festival of Lights (Chanukah)

Chanukah, or Festival of Lights, lasts for eight days, and occurs in November or December. Every night a candle in the menorah (candle-holder) is lit in honor of the Maccabees, who recaptured the temple in Jerusalem from the Syrians in 165 B.C.

Games are played and gifts exchanged.

Cut a paper pattern (on the fold) of a **menorah**. (See Figure 4-1.) Use *9" x 12"* or *12" x 18" paper*, depending on size wanted. Trace pattern (folded) on two pieces of folded *waxed paper*, and cut out.

Figure 4-1

77

Scrape bits of *scrap crayons* in different colors onto one of the waxed paper menorahs (in open position). Lay other one on top and iron, so that crayon bits melt and are "laminated" between the two sheets. Iron on and between sheets (to form a pad) of *newspaper*.

Display mounted or unmounted, or put on windows with *clear tape*.

Napkin candles can be used as part of a table setting.

Fold any *paper napkin* (white or colored) into a triangular shape, keeping the folded edge towards you. Fold this bottom edge up about an inch. Turn the napkin over. Starting at the left edge, roll the entire napkin into a narrow cylinder shape. Tuck end into the fold, and stand up. (See Figure 4-2A, 4-2B, and 4-2C.)

Figure 4-2A

Figure 4-2B

Figure 4-2C

Figure 4-3

The tip can be colored to resemble a flame.

Cloth napkins can be made into candles, too!

Design candles look best when done on *manila drawing paper*.

Crayon a "leaded" look design within a large candle shape. (See Figure 4-3.)

Abstract shapes separated by thick black lines produce interesting results. Crayon heavily and cut out.

Rub a little *salad oil* on the back, using a *paper towel* or *napkin*. Luminosity, if not complete transparency, creates a different type of window decoration.

Mount on windows with *clear tape*. Roll pieces of tape with sticky side out and place between window and candle. Use the same procedure with clear or *masking tape* whenever a window display is called for, so that tape is not visible.

St. Nicholas Day (European Festivities)

St. Nicholas Day is December 6th. It is celebrated in Belgium and in other European nations. There are festivities and children receive gifts on this date rather than on Christmas Day.

Paper wreaths can be made large or small, used to decorate doors or attached to Christmas greeting cards or gifts.

Tear irregular shapes of *red* and *green paper* and paste, overlapping, into a wreath shape. Torn paper berries or a bow can be added.

Younger children might find it easier to paste the shapes onto a pre-cut paper wreath (doughnut) shape. Be sure the shape is completely covered. (See Figure 4-4.)

Figure 4-4

For the cut paper variation, stack *red* and *green papers* (*poster* or *construction*) and cut enough leaf shapes to make the wreath.

Both versions take time to complete, so shapes should not be very small.

Brown 12" x 18" construction paper and *thick white tempera paint* are the ingredients needed for the creation of **gingerbread cookies.**

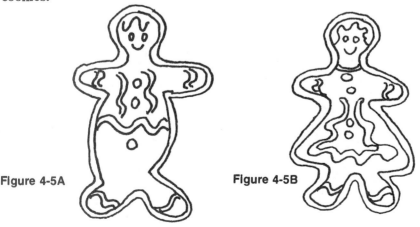

Figure 4-5A   **Figure 4-5B**

Draw a large boy/girl rounded cookie figure with *chalk*. (See Figures 4-5A and 4-5B.)

White paint in a *squeeze dispenser* is used for the icing details, such as buttons, features, and other trimmings. A *thin brush* or *pencil* can also be used. Icing can be applied all around the cookie.

Cut out and hang up on tree or wall.

Double-folded cookies can become greeting cards. Mini-cookies can be used as gift tags.

Human Rights Day

Human Rights Day, December 10, is an official United Nations holiday, by Presidential Proclamation No. 2866 of December 6, 1949.

The making of **torn paper portraits** (Figure 4-6) is an easy way to introduce youngsters to the recognition of the planes and contours necessary in drawing faces.

Figure 4-6

Student models can be used, if desired.

Otherwise, begin with a torn oval shape in any color. Tear contrasting colored pieces of paper, and build upon the oval base.

Shadows and highlights, eye and nose placement, hair line, size of neck, etc., should all be discussed.

A demonstration lesson prior to this activity would be valuable.

Results will have an irregular or jagged look because of the torn edges, but this type of experimentation can free the student to try some other approaches to portrait drawing.

Wright Brothers Day (First Flight at Kitty Hawk)

Wright Brothers Day is December 17 by Presidential proclamation. The first successful airplane flight was at Kitty Hawk, North Carolina, in the year 1903.

If some children already know how to make an **origami airplane**, let them assist others who experience difficulty.

Fold *9" x 12" poster paper* (in *any color*) in half. Keep the fold at the top.

Beginning at the left side, fold up the bottom to meet the top fold three times. Do this on both sides. (See Figures 4-7A–4-7D.)

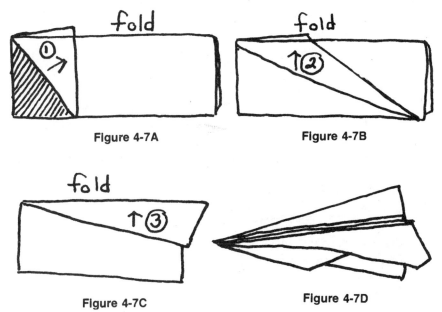

Figure 4-7A

Figure 4-7B

Figure 4-7C

Figure 4-7D

Plane can be decorated with crayon designs.

Tape together on the underside, grasp, and fly it. It is safer to fly these planes outdoors!

For a **wire outline plane**, bend *two lightweight wire hangers* into a basic airplane shape. (See Figure 4-8.)

Clear tape in a few strategic places will hold it together.

Pieces of *flexible wire* and a *long-nosed pliers* can be aids in this process.

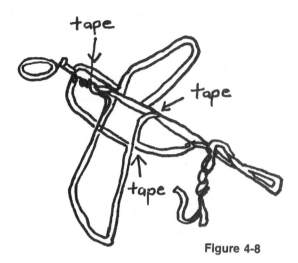

Figure 4-8

Twisting and cutting of wire, if necessary for variations, should be done with care.

Cover any open sections with *tissue paper* in *assorted colors*. Cut larger than the space to be covered, overlap, and secure with *white glue*.

Several layers of tissue can be glued together for added strength. These pieces can also become additions, such as engines or propeller, to the airplane.

Some children might want to add *cardboard rolls* or score *cardboard pieces* to simulate exhausts, etc.

Identifying insignia or stars of tissue paper can be glued on for interest.

Masking tape can also be used easily and successfully to cover the open sections, instead of tissue paper. It can be left uncolored, or colored with *brown* or *black marker*.

Imaginative results might be both old fashioned *and* futuristic planes!

Pilgrims Landed

Figure 4-9

The Pilgrims landed at Plymouth Rock on December 21st in 1620. Forefathers' Day has been observed, mainly in New England, since 1769.

Pilgrim children pictures can be made in honor of this day. (See Figure 4-9.)

Black and *white construction paper* is cut into simple geometric shapes (oval, rectangle, square, etc.) and "assembled" on *12" x 18" gray paper* for the background.

Portions of the gray paper become part of the body.

Belt buckle is a cut paper letter "O."

The hat can be the origami "cup" described in November's lesson, "Paper Cup Pilgrim Heads."

Winter Begins

Winter begins on the 21st or 22nd of December. The sun is farthest from the equator on this day of winter solstice.

Children can bring in *twigs* or small *sections* of *branches* to be used as models for **drawing from nature** in *pen* and *ink*. (See Figure 4-10.)

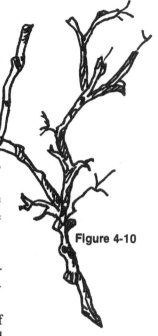

Figure 4-10

Details can be studied closely, using this approach.

Additions to the drawings should be encouraged, and compositions can be created by repetition of one twig or branch, or utilization of several.

A twig itself can be used as the drawing instrument, instead of a pen. Differences in control and results can then be compared and discussed.

If possible, outdoor observations and on-site drawings would be valuable if realism is the goal.

Christmas

Christmas Day, December 25, is celebrated throughout the United States, its territories, and the Christian world. The American celebration is centered around gift-giving and a decorated tree.

Before 1840, it was strictly a religious holiday. Customs, all commemorative of the birth of Christ, vary from country to country.

It is the last holiday of the year, but to many the most important.

A clean *tin* or *aluminum can* can become a sturdy body for a **Santa Claus figure**. (See Figure 4-11.)

Cover with *red felt* or *paper* cut to size, and glue on.

For this "sitting" Santa, add long strips of *stiff red* or *white*

Figure 4-11

. *paper* to the inside bottom of the can. Add *black cut paper* boots to ends of the strips.

Fold strips back and forth if you want legs to be bouncy.

Add strips (for arms) to the middle of the can, along with cut paper hands or mittens.

Belt, buckle, buttons, etc., complete the body.

The head and hat, also of stiff paper, can be trimmed with *cotton* and glued on to top center of can.

Perch on desk or table, and let legs dangle.

This Santa can be filled with candy canes or other Christmas treats, and taken home after a class party.

Directions for a **reindeer paper hand puppet** (Figure 4-12) are as follows:

Fold a sheet of *12" x 18" light gray construction* or other paper into *thirds*, the *long* way.

Fold down about five inches from the top. This becomes the head (face).

For the nose, fold in sides, on an angle, as shown in Figure 4-12.

Staple, tape, or paste down on the back of face.

Figure 4-12

Staple or tape the sides of the reindeer, but leave the bottom and inside open so hand can be inserted for manipulation.

Decorate with fringed paper hair, antlers, scored paper ears, etc.

A piece of *wool* and/or a real little bell makes a nice "lead" when tied around the center. It can, however, be drawn on with a marker.

Mini-reindeer, made the same way, can be hung from a Christmas tree.

Any combination of *red*, *white* or *green 12" x 18" construction paper* can be used to make a **lace-up Santa boot** (Figure 4-13.)

Trace or draw a simple boot or stocking shape on one sheet. Cut two of them at one time (by putting one paper on top of another), so boot can be laced and filled with candy.

Punch holes with a paper *punch* all around the boot, except for the top.

Lace together with suitable color *wool* or *string*. Use fingers or a *needle* with a large eye. When finished, tie on the inside, to secure. Leave the top open.

Add *cotton* or *white paper* for a fluffy top. Paste on Christmas

Figure 4-13

symbols, like small trees, balls or bells, in contrasting colors. Both sides can be decorated.

To personalize, have the children write or print their first names with markers, on the top of the boot.

Washington's Crossing of the Delaware

George Washington crossed the Delaware River on December 25, 1776. He and his half-frozen army reached Trenton at daybreak and captured the Hessians.

This historic event can be used as the subject of an interesting art project, **negative-positive pull-apart prints**. (See Figure 4-14.)

Figure 4-14

This project involves the liberal use of paint. Some paints are multipurpose, and have the consistency of finger paint or thick tempera. Experiment to see which paint gives the best results.

Spoon *three* different *paint* colors onto a sheet of *12" x 18" construction paper* in any color. Have the children spread the paint downward until the paper is almost covered. A "frame" can be left around the edges. Colors will overlap into each other when spread.

Be sure to tell children to spread paint with the hand they do not write with.

Overlay a second sheet of construction paper on the first.

Next draw a scene, with a pencil, of Washington's crossing. Prepare for this lesson with pictures, accounts and discussions of this event.

Press hard enough so paint is "etched" through. Do not lift up top paper during drawing.

Pull the papers apart carefully. Two prints will be in evidence. Both "positive" and "negative" prints can be enhanced with paper frames. Put up an exhibit of all the prints.

Black paper and *white paint* also create exciting prints.

New Year's Eve

New Year's Eve is December 31st. Celebrations are tinged with sadness, as the "old" year is ushered out in preparation for the new one.

A time "countdown" is traditionally held at Times Square in New York City, and all over the world people wait to shout "Happy New Year!"

Party hats make any occasion more festive, and children will enjoy making some to wear on New Year's Eve.

Begin with a cone shape, made of *12" x 18" construction paper*. Make cone one of two ways: cut a half-circle from the paper, bend ends until they meet (hold paper with straight side of half-circle on top); or hold paper on the 18" side, bring corners together, and staple. (See Figures 4-15A and 4-15B.)

Figure 4-15A

Figure 4-15B

Edges can be cut into points, if desired. (See Figure 4-15C.)

Use *shiny paper, tinfoil*, etc., to decorate. Cut and fringe long rectangular strips in assorted colors, and staple all around the hat, overlapping each section. (See Figure 4-15D.)

A bouncy *spiral* or *fringe* of *paper* can be inserted into the top of the hat.

For a spiral, begin at any point on a circle, and continue cutting all around. (See Figure 4-15E.)

Spirals can be pasted or stapled all over the hat, too!

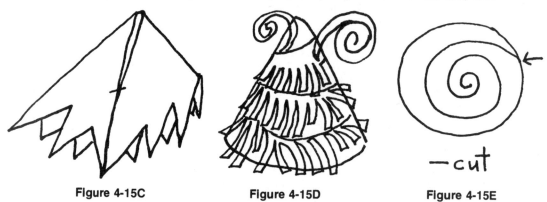

Figure 4-15C   Figure 4-15D   Figure 4-15E

Bonus Activities for December

Rudyard Kipling's Birthday

Rudyard Kipling, English poet and novelist, was born in Bombay, India, on December 30, 1865. He died in London on January 18, 1936. He was the author of the *Jungle Book*.

Torn paper jungle animals would be an ideal lesson after a trip to the zoo or circus. (See Figure 4-16.)

Stories by Kipling can be read, and pictures and films shown prior to this activity.

Use *paper paste* and *large sheets* of *paper* in colors appropriate for animals. Tearing aids spontaneity, and the irregularity of the torn edges adds interest. Tell the children to eliminate any straight edges.

Tear large shapes for bodies; build the rest of the beast(s) with proportionately smaller torn pieces.

Figure 4-16

A teacher demonstration might help.

Children should be encouraged to try both realistic and imaginary creatures.

Discussions of thickness of neck, legs, trunk, etc., would be helpful.

A torn paper mural entitled **Animal Parade** might be one result or culminating activity, if interest is high.

Many classroom teachers stretch a wire or fasten a taut string high across the room at the beginning of the school year. It is handy for hanging pictures and mobiles, and serves as additional display space. This helps especially when bulletin board space is limited. Be sure to hang it high enough so it does not interfere with children's vision or movement in the room.

Attach large, colorful paper leaves of *sturdy paper* to real *tree branches* and suspend from *wire hangers*. (See Figure 4-17.)

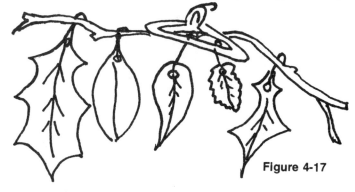

Figure 4-17

Wire or clear (or colored) tape can be used to fasten the branch(es) to the hanger(s).

Punch and string the leaves so they can move with the breeze!

Have children select branches that are interesting and not too thick or heavy.

Try employment of different themes for these mobiles. In keeping with the Kipling spirit, hang paper jungle animals, too!

5

 **HIGHLIGHTS**
of the month of
JANUARY

New Year's Day

Tournament of Roses

Betsy Ross' Birthday

Captain John Smith Captured by Indians

First U. S. Balloon Flight

Martin Luther King's Birthday

Benjamin Franklin's Birthday

John Hancock's Birthday

Gold Discovered in California

Snow Days

Birthday of the Author of *Winnie-the-Pooh*

New Year's Day

New Year's Day, January 1st, is a legal holiday in all states and territories. Julius Caesar designated January first as the beginning of the year, changing it from early March.

Celebrations are varied—from the Rose Bowl football game in Pasadena, California, to the parade of Mummers in Philadelphia.

We make resolutions, and think of both the past year and the one ahead of us.

An interesting activity is to sketch large simple outline shapes of **Father Time and Baby New Year**, the two familiar symbols representative of the passage of time. (See Figure 5-1.)

A supply of *magazines* in the classroom comes in handy for this and for many art activities. Research would include pictures of elderly gentlemen and babies, which should be relatively easy to locate.

Cut small shapes from *colorful magazine pages* and fill in outline sketch(es).

Use *black* and *white print sections* for faces so figures will be easily recognizable. *Marker* "touches" can be employed for clarity.

Other symbols may be added: top hat, horn, clock, banner, scythe.

Paste on a *white paper background*.

Figure 5-1

Tournament of Roses

The Pasadena Tournament of Roses, in operation since 1866, is an association that produces a beautiful parade featuring a display of rose-covered floats of all kinds and colors. Shapes and figures are also constructed of roses.

To make **roses in the classroom,** use *red, pink, white* or *yellow 12" x 18" construction paper.* Make a paper (*oaktag*) pattern. (See Figure 5-2A.)

Trace as many as you want, one on a sheet. Wind up, beginning with the narrow end, and staple together to get a beautiful, rose-like shape. (See Figure 5-2B.)

If shape is not wholly pleasing, cut out small triangular nicks at random to improve the look of the petals.

Try some roses made of *tissue paper*, also.

They can be stapled to a background. Stem and leaves can be crayoned.

Single flowers are created by the addition of *green florist wire* or *pipe cleaner* and *green tissue* or *cut paper* leaves. Inserted into a

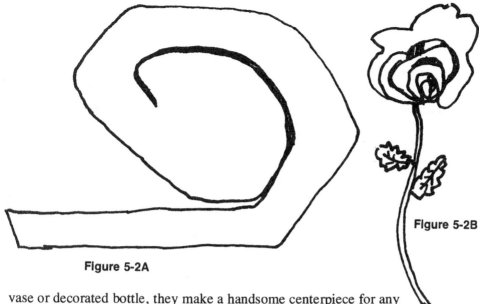

Figure 5-2A

Figure 5-2B

vase or decorated bottle, they make a handsome centerpiece for any table!

Everything from vitamins to vinegar is packaged attractively today. Children can bring in different *glass containers* and trade them.

Gather *rose petals*, preferably in the morning, and dry them carefully on paper for several days. Spread and stir once in a while so air can aid drying.

Layer them in the recycled jar(s), *salt*ing lightly. Top with a *mixture of spices* containing any combination of cloves, thyme, anise, bay leaves, peppermint, cinnamon, allspice, ground mace and orrisroot (from the drugstore).

Continue layering until jar is full. Remove lid only when scent is wanted.

For more color, add dried petals of other flowers. Dried or ground lemon or orange peel can be extra ingredients. Tonka beans add the aroma of vanilla; fragrant oils enhance the mixture.

The resultant **potpourri jar** can be kept in any room or closet, or the mixture can be tied into cloth for sachets.

Betsy Ross' Birthday

Betsy Ross (1752–1836) was the maker of the first American flag. She was a seamstress from Philadelphia who executed the flag's design from a sketch submitted to her by a committee appointed by Congress. We celebrate her birthday on January first.

Reproduce the **Flag of 1776** on *unbleached muslin* or *sheeting*. (See Figure 5-3.)

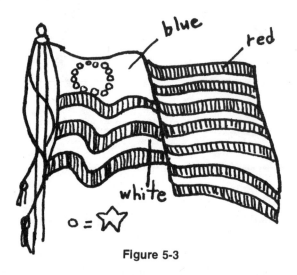

Figure 5-3

Individual flags can be done on smaller pieces of the same material and stitched together for an unusual wall hanging. Turn the top down and sew onto a *dowel stick*.

Either way, sketch on with pencil and color with a heavy application of *crayon*.

If you choose to make it washable, iron between *pads* of *newspaper* to "set." Color should show through on the back.

Some ambitious students might like to recreate other memorable flags: Grand Union, Pine Tree, Rattlesnake, Bennington, or the 1812 Star-Spangled Banner. Pictures can be found in dictionaries, history books, magazines, etc.

Captain John Smith Captured by Indians

Captain John Smith was captured by the Indians on January 5th, 1608. Legend tells us he was saved from death by Pocahontas, daughter of the Indian chief Powhatan.

To make an **Indian face**, bend a *wire hanger* into a diamond shape, leaving the curved top piece for hanging up. (See Figure 5-4.)

Figure 5-4

Stretch an old *stocking* around this frame and knot near the top to secure.

Trim stocking with *pasted felt pieces* for the face, and add (staple) lengths of *cotton roving* for hair. Insert a real *chicken feather* near the top for additional "fillip"!

First U.S. Balloon Flight

The first United States balloon flight was on January 9th, 1793. Jean-Pierre Blanchard of Philadelphia made the ascent, watched by President George Washington and a large crowd.

In the years that followed, ballooning became an international sport.

Many children have seen clowns and performers create **balloon animals**.

A large box (gross) of *long jumbo balloons* is relatively inexpensive.

Experiment with funny figures and animals.

Blow up several, tie off with *string*, and twist some of the balloons gently in the center, creating two sections. Twist two of these together for a body and two legs. Twist some balloons into three sections.

Continue in the same way, adding balloons until an animal is created. (See Figures 5-5A and 5-5B.)

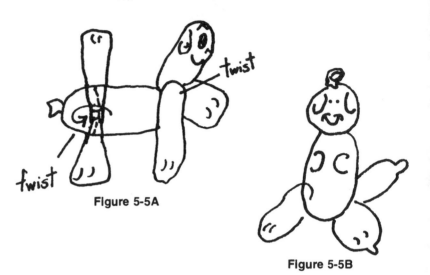

Figure 5-5A

Figure 5-5B

Figure 5-6

Manipulate so tail and head are up.

Sit some animals upright.

Marker or *ballpoint pen* faces and details should be applied carefully, so balloons do not break.

Balloons of good quality can lessen the frustration of air leakage and will not burst as easily.

Balloon string spheres add a festive note to any classroom. You do not need a holiday to enjoy them! (See Figure 5-6.)

Dip pre-cut lengths of *assorted colored string* in *white glue* thinned with water.

Wrap strings randomly around an *inflated round balloon*. Leave some spaces if you want a lacy effect. Let dry thoroughly, prick balloon and pull it out.

Spread a little glue and sprinkle with glitter for a shimmery effect.

Suspend from overhead lights with string. Make several, trying balloons of different shapes and sizes.

Some can be all one color. Create a color scheme by hanging in a predetermined order.

Martin Luther King's Birthday

Martin Luther King's birthday is January 15th. He was born in 1929 and died on April 4, 1968. Dr. King was an American civil rights leader and winner of the Nobel Peace Prize.

To honor King, make a mobile of **figures from black history.**

Cut a long spiral from a *circle of 12" x 18" construction paper* in the color of your choice. For spiral-cutting directions, see December, "Paper Cone Party Hats." Do not cut the spiral too thin.

Punch holes at varying points on the spiral, including one at the top for hanging.

An alternate method would be the use of a *dowel stick* or *wire hanger,* tied with different lengths of *string* or *wire.* Tie carefully for proper balance when hung.

Draw and cut out small profile silhouettes from *stiff black paper.* Source materials will yield the names of several important people: Henry Ossawa Tanner, Sojourner Truth, Isaac Myers, Lorraine Hansberry, Charles S. Johnson, Whitney M. Young, Jr., Williams Wells Brown, Blanche K. Bruce, Ferdinand "Jelly Roll" Morton, Granville T. Woods, Isaac Murphy, Frances Ellen Watkins Harper, Crispus Attucks and others.

Punch and string the profiles and attach to the hanging devices.

Younger children can use cut-out pictures of faces collected from magazines and newspapers. Pictures can be pasted on both sides of stiff paper.

For a **woven silhouette** of King (Figure 5-7), draw (or trace) and cut out a simple head in profile from *12" x 18" paper.* Poke scissors, cutting straight lines across the face (horizontally), about an inch apart.

Cut one-inch strips in a contrasting color and weave through, in and out, until a checkerboard look is obtained. *Black* and *white* make an effective combination.

Strips for weaving can be straight or wavy. The "loom" (profile) lines can be uneven, also. This will result in an "op-art" look.

Cut off strips so they do not show beyond the silhouette and paste down on the back.

Rule off lines at random on *white paper* for **mosaic silhouettes**, having traced profile beforehand. Then color in the spaces created with *red* and *blue crayons*, leaving some spaces white. *Oil crayons* create a "brighter" look.

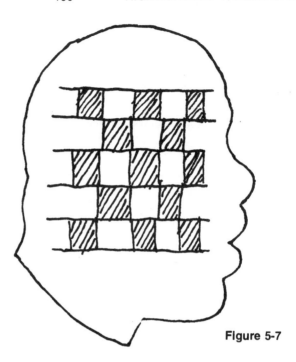

Figure 5-7

The silhouette can also be filled in (pasted on) with *red* and *blue* or *black cut paper* pieces to resemble a mosaic. Again, leave some of the white paper background showing.

Overlap the pieces entirely, or leave a space between each piece to simulate grout—the white plaster in real mosaics.

Benjamin Franklin's Birthday

Benjamin Franklin was born on January 17th, 1706, and died April 17th, 1790. He was a famous American statesman, inventor, philosopher, scientist and writer.

He discovered electricity in lightning, invented the lightning rod and printed *Poor Richard's Almanack*, which contained wise and witty sayings.

There are a great many simple **printing techniques**.

Cut a *potato* in half. Teachers can help in cutting a simple design into one half with a small knife. Draw on with a pencil first, and cut away the excess. The raised part will print. Dip into *tempera paint* (creamy consistency) and press onto various papers: news-print, tissue, etc. Printing inks can be tried, also.

You can also make simple cuts *into* the surface of the potato, or just use the potato half itself as a printing instrument.

Press a small ball of *clay* (regular or non-hardening) into a pancake shape. Incise a simple design with a pencil, pen point, nail, etc. Coat with paint, and press. Try several patterns of "repeat" designs to make original greeting cards or wrapping paper.

Sponges, kitchen tools (potato masher, etc.), built-up cardboard shapes and pipe cleaners (bent at one end) can be used in a similar way to create varied prints.

String and *glue* are good for **outline prints**.

Arrange pieces of *string* on a pre-drawn figure shape on *cardboard*. (See Figure 5-8.)

Figure 5-8

Older children can move string around to get detailed contour line figures without pre-drawing. They can also try creating continuous line figures from one piece of string.

Glue (squeeze on) in place. Let dry. Print with conventional *inks, water based* (for easy clean-up) or *oil based*.

Try some abstract designs. The glue itself and the texture of the strings will lead to interesting "organic" looking results that will be a surprise!

Discarded *cookie tins* can hold the inks for rolling on the *brayers*.

There are several types of prepared printing materials on the market. Some require cutting and have a pre-gummed backing; others are spongy, and can be drawn on with a pencil.

Experimentation with different methods and materials is a good introduction to other, more sophisticated printing techniques, like linoleum block, wood cut, silk-screen, lithography and etching.

Miniature kites (Figure 5-9) make great favors.

Begin with a 3″ x 3″ square of *brightly colored origami paper* or *wallpaper samples*. Turn so one of the corners is at the top, creating a diamond shape. Fold in both sides so they meet.

Fold top down; then re-open. Paste on small crosspieces of *light balsa wood, popsicle sticks* or *twigs,* for an added touch of realism. Finish with a *string* and a tail of gayly *colored papers* or small pieces of *scrap material*.

Larger versions can be made and flown outdoors.

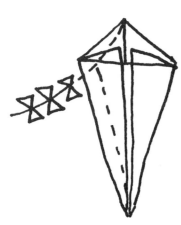

Figure 5-9

John Hancock's Birthday

John Hancock's birth anniversary is January 23rd. He was an American statesman and patriot who was the first signer of the Declaration of Independence. Born in 1739, he died on October 8, 1793.

For a **class signature scroll**, upper grades can try some fancy calligraphy; lower grades can practice handwriting.

Study reproductions of important historical documents for this group project.

Result can be a nice keepsake for the teacher, and double as a year-round display on a bulletin board.

Pen and *ink* should be used. Experiment first with *different* sizes of *pen points*. Upper grades can use *indelible inks*.

A class credo can be developed and signed.

Try *heavy brown paper* torn at the edges to simulate antique paper. Crumple and open again to "age" the paper. Iron between sheets of *newspaper*. It can be burned slightly at the torn edges (under teacher supervision), or darkened with *brown crayon* or *oil pastel*.

Roll and tie with a ribbon, or mount and display when completed.

Fancy, heavy papers in gold or silver would also produce a dramatic effect. The teacher should sign his/her name also!

Rub-on transfer letters in fancy script or gold leaf papers (available in stationery and art supply stores) might be interesting to try, too.

Gold Discovered in California

Gold was discovered by James Wilson Marshall at Sutter's Mill, California on the 24th of January, 1848. The search for this precious metal captured the imagination of many. Men flocked to establish gold claims. By 1849, a large scale gold rush was underway. San Francisco grew from a small town to a city of 25,000 people in one year.

Many items (cookies, greeting cards) are packaged in *boxes* with see-through *plastic lids*. Save them for an activity based on **gold fever**.

Use *tempera paint* (mixed with *detergent* for adhesion) or paper to cover any lettering. Decorate the outside to resemble small television sets by adding dials, an antenna, and knobs.

Inside, set up miniature figures or cut paper people engaged in scenes of the old gold fever days. Books will yield ideas.

Candy coins, wrapped in gold foil, would be effective. Search for gold papers to be used in creating these dioramas.

Bonus Activities for January

Snow Days

Many people have never seen snow, since it falls on only about one-third of the earth's surface.

In the temperate zone, snow falls in winter. Weather records show that the average annual snowfall has remained the same since the last half of the 1800's. Yet new snowfall records are set almost every year.

Dramatic **snow scenes** can be made on *black, 12" x 18"* (or larger) *construction paper*. A *cotton swab* is used instead of a brush.

Look outdoors on a snowy day for inspiration, or, if you live in a part of the country where it doesn't snow, look at pictures of snow scenes. Fill *paint cups* with *creamy white tempera paint* so children can work individually.

Children should be encouraged to paint freely and quickly. No preliminary drawing is required.

When one end of the swab is thoroughly saturated, simply turn and use the other end.

Clean-up is easy. Collect used swabs in a piece of newspaper, wrap up and throw away.

Be sure to remind children to incorporate part of the background paper in their paintings. For example, a snowman's eyes, nose, mouth, buttons and inside portion of hat will be the black background paper, and must be imagined beforehand.

This kind of one-color painting can be an aid in the teaching of negative and positive concepts.

Skiers, snowflakes, snowballs, snowbanks, skaters, trees and telephone poles laden with snow will appear in these scenes.

A gentle hint can be made to young artists—too many ''polka dot'' snowflakes will weaken and obscure the paintings.

Figure 5-10

Large or small **snowman mobiles** (Figure 5-10) liven up a dull January day.

Construct from *two white paper circles*: one large for the body, one smaller for the head. Very young children can use lids to trace the circles.

To simplify, draw the hat and the head together and cut out in one piece.

Punch at top of hat, bottom of face and top of body. Add *string*(s) to hang up and to connect head to the body. Be sure to leave some slack so body can move with the breeze.

Decorate with *black markers* or *crayon* on both sides. Add a face, mittens, buttons and a belt.

Staple a *tissue paper* scarf in a bright color to the bottom of the head.

For a cute little **3-D snowman** figure, crumple *two* balls of *newspaper*—a larger one for the body, a smaller one for the head.

Wrap up in a larger piece of household *tinfoil* to cover. Mold with your hands. Be sure the newspaper balls are completely covered.

Decorate with a folded rectangular piece of *tissue paper* for a scarf and *black construction paper* pasted details (face, buttons, etc.). Use *white glue*.

Stand the snowman on your desk for a winter companion!

Magazine snowflakes can be hung up as mobiles, pasted onto backgrounds, or used as folder cover decorations.

Cut circles (any size) from large colorful *magazine pages*. Use a compass, trace the *lid* of a large *coffee can*, or draw freehand.

Fold three times. Snip off sections with fancy scissor cuts, making sure portions of the folds are left intact in several places so snowflake does not fall apart. (See Figure 5-11.)

– fold

Figure 5-11

If you cut deeply into the center, you will get an eight-pointed snowflake.

Each one will be different.

Younger children can fold the circle twice, for a round snowflake.

Birthday of the Author of *Winnie-the-Pooh*

A. A. Milne was the English author of *Winnie-the-Pooh*, a children's classic.

He was born on January 18, 1882, and died in 1956.

A **paper stuffed teddy bear** makes a wonderful toy. (See Figure 5-12.)

Draw a simple outline shape of a jumbo teddy bear on *18" x 24" manila paper*. Keep the ears, the arms and the legs thick and wide.

Figure 5-12

Slip another, same size sheet of manila paper under it, and cut out two of these shapes.

Color (*brown*) a back and a front heavily on the sides that will be visible. Color before stuffing.

A heavy application of waxed crayon adds strength to the paper. Try coloring for texture, so bear looks fuzzy.

Blend *yellow* crayon with the brown for round, paw-like shapes. Use *black* crayon to add a happy face.

Stuff lightly with *newspaper* or crumpled *manila scraps* left over after cutting out the bear.

Staple half the bear and begin to stuff. Continue until bear is filled and stapled all around.

Punch top of head; string and hang, or take home to play with.

What a nice surprise for a younger child to receive!

6

 **HIGHLIGHTS**

of the month of

FEBRUARY

Groundhog Day

Negro History Week

Chinese New Year

Mardi Gras

Lincoln's Birthday

Valentine's Day

National Brotherhood Week

Washington's Birthday

Boy Scout Day

Daniel Boone's Birthday

Purim

Lantern Festival (End of Chinese New Year)

Groundhog Day

Groundhog Day is February 2nd. An old belief says if the groundhog sees his shadow on this day when he emerges from his hole, there will be six more weeks of winter. The woodchuck, a small rodent, was named "groundhog" by the Pilgrims.

Shadow pictures (Figure 6-1) double the viewer's interest!

Figure 6-1

Using *gray 12" x 18" construction paper* for the background and *black* and *white* for the elements of the picture, cut two of everything.

Use an outline or silhouette approach. Cut people, flowers, trees, animals, etc., so they can be recognized by their outlines without any additional markings or adornments. Arrangement is important. Leave a border around the edges of the gray paper.

Paste so both figures, etc., are visible, overlapping slightly.

The monochromatic scheme is effective; others can be tried.

Negro History Week

February 9th to 15th is designated as Negro History Week. It includes Abraham Lincoln's birthday and commemorates events in American Negro history.

Some famous names to be honored are listed in the January chapter under "Martin Luther King's Birthday," in the section that deals with making a mobile of figures from black history. Children can make a **picture gallery** of these people or of historical events in which they were involved.

Some soda cans are held by a continuous *strip* of six *clear plastic circles*. Cut corresponding size *paper circles* in a *light color*. Draw pictures or events or cut from *magazines* and *newspapers* and paste onto the paper circles. Staple into the plastic "frames." (See Figure 6-2.)

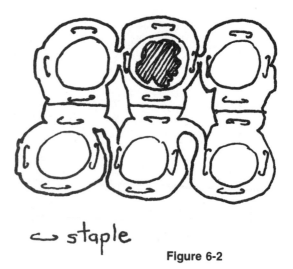

⌒ staple

Figure 6-2

The clear plastic holder can be colored with *black markers* first. Several holders can be stapled together to form a long continuous strip.

In another project, children can make **paper frames for famous people** in any size needed.

One easy way: cut into a *12" x 18" sheet* of *construction paper* in your choice of color. Cut in a wavy fashion, going deeply into the four corners (Figure 6-3A.)

Slip appropriate size picture to be framed underneath, and paste or staple. The corners can be bent slightly, on the diagonal, for a dimensional effect.

Another method: begin with needed size rectangle. Draw lines for a box within this rectangle. Repeat, drawing a second box (Figure 6-3B.)

Starting at the lines for the smallest inside box, rule off two diagonal lines (Figure 6-3C.)

Cut on these lines, making sure to poke scissors on the lines carefully, so nothing is cut away.

Open these four triangular flaps, fold back and paste down (Figure 3-6D.)

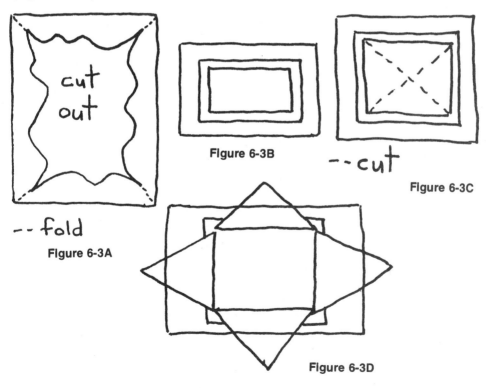

Figure 6-3B

Figure 6-3C

Figure 6-3A

Figure 6-3D

If you prefer, leave folded flaps unpasted for a "shadow box" look.

To re-use this frame, tape picture (at the four corners) to be mounted on the back, Picture should be slightly larger than the opening.

Remove and replace with other pictures of the same size.

"Mini-frames," 4" x 6" or smaller, make good backgrounds for magazine pictures of interest.

For another simple frame, cut diagonally into the corners of a square, bend up and over and paste.

Chinese New Year

Chinese New Year begins on or about February 11th. It is celebrated for 28 days, according to dates from the ancient Chinese calendar. A cycle is twelve years. Years are designated with the names of animals, like rabbit, tiger, mouse, dog, pig, rooster, monkey, etc.

Look at pictures, puzzles and animal crackers to get some ideas for simple **animal outline shapes**.

Children should try drawing several, using *manila paper*, until they have a few satisfactory ones to cut out and use for rubbings.

Place one cut paper animal under a *long strip* of *newsprint* or *construction paper*. Peel outside wrapper from a *crayon* in color desired.

Rub firmly on the paper, going beyond the shape, so entire outline will appear. Lift shape, move it under the paper to another position and repeat the procedure until the end of the paper is reached. Hold the crayon flat against the paper when rubbing.

One-color/one-animal repeat designs seem to be most successful, but different colors and animals might be preferred by some children.

Explain that some additional lines outside the animal shape add to the rubbing's charm. However, the entire background paper should not be covered with color.

An animal design or pattern can be created, or a straight-line "parade."

Look for readings on the Chinese calendar to find out which animal represents your birthdate.

In another project, young children can make **Chinese sun hats** from a *circle* of *15" x 18" manila paper.*

It is easy to trace the bottom of your classroom trash can.

Cut out the circle; then cut one slit into the center (Figure 6-4A).

Decorate with made-up squiggles to look like Chinese characters. Use *black crayon* or *markers.*

Overlap the slit sides and staple or paste, to form a conical, pointed hat. Punch both sides and add *strings* to tie under chin (Figure 6-4B).

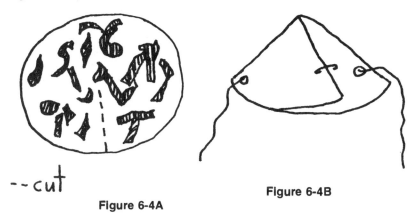

Figure 6-4A

Figure 6-4B

Mardi Gras

Mardi Gras, which precedes Lent, is celebrated in New Orleans, Louisiana, Mobile, Alabama and certain Florida and Mississippi cities. It is the last feast before Lent. Two weeks of celebration include parades and masked balls.

To make **Mardi Gras masks,** cut a light-bulb shape from folded *18" x 24" manila* or *stiffer paper.* (See Figure 6-5.)

Cut out shapes for nose and mouth on the fold, and poke scissors for eye hole(s) and other design shapes.

Open and complete by outlining (contour line approach) the open spaces in *crayon* or other medium and adding any other details.

Top off the mask with cut paper, raffia, string, etc., for hair.

The masks can be ''scary'' or funny.

Display, rather than wear, these large decorative masks.

Figure 6-5

You can make **masks into mobiles**, too! Make up an interesting shape on *flexible paper*, such as that used for origami. Draw an oval on the inside and cut out, leaving top attached to the outside shape. Fold the oval and cut eyes, nose and mouth. (See Figure 6-6.)

Figure 6-6

Figure 6-7

Push out eyes and nose so they stand away from the face. Fold and flex top of oval so face stands away from the outside shape, or frame.

Fringe strips of paper for hair and staple. Ears can also be attached. Punch top; string and hang.

Lincoln's Birthday

Abraham Lincoln's birthday is February 12th, and it is observed on this date in most states. Lincoln was the 16th President of the United States. Born in 1809, he died in Washington, D. C. on April 15, 1865.

To make **Lincoln log cabins**, save individual *milk cartons* (half-pint size) and rinse out.

Staple top in unopened position to form a roof. On one of the short sides, cut an opening for a door. (See Figure 6-7.)

Roll small (about ½″ x 3″) *light brown butcher paper* into log-like segments. Paste each one together.

Line (*mucilage* or *white glue*) entire carton with these small cylindrical logs until completely covered (except for bottom).

Some logs may have to be cut smaller to fit certain sections.

Cabin can then be decorated with *brown crayon* markings that suggest knotholes in wood.

Cut a slit in the side and fill with Lincoln pennies.

Valentine's Day

St. Valentine's Day is February 14. It celebrates the festival of two saints martyred by the Roman Emperor Claudius II, over 1700 years ago.

Thousands of years ago, the Romans honored a god thought to protect them from wolves. They gave a party for this god, and noticed that the birds seemed to choose mates on this day. They decided then to give gifts and love letters to their sweethearts. The custom persists to this day.

An interesting project for St. Valentine's Day is the making of **bread dough heart pendants**, which are enjoyable to make, wear, and give as gifts.

The recipe is: 6 slices of crumbled *bread* with crusts removed, 6 teaspoons of white glue, ½ teaspoon of *glycerine* or *liquid detergent*.

Knead until pliable. Make up more individual batches if necessary. Do not double the recipe.

If you prefer, use baker's clay. Try both if interest is keen and time permits.

Recipes vary somewhat, but general directions for baker's clay are as follows:

Mix 4 cups of *flour* with 1 cup of *salt*. Slowly add 1½–1¾ cups of hot *water*.

Knead on a floured board for 5–20 minutes until smooth. Add flour if mixture is sticky, water if too stiff. Bake at 325–350° for 1–2 hours until light brown and hard. Cool. A small *toaster-broiler oven* works well in school.

Shape mixture into several small hearts on a cookie sheet or the broiler pan. Poke a hole at the top with a nail or pencil point so heart(s) can be strung with *wool*, *leather* or *string* and worn around the neck. A key chain can be made by adding beaded links from the hardware or dime store.

Seal hearts with a *plastic polymer medium*. Paint with *red* or *pink* (mix red and white) *acrylic paint*, using small brushes. Spray or apply a sealer of *gloss fixative* or medium.

Tempera paint and *shellac* can be used as a substitute.

In another activity, **crayon resist valentines** with a Pennsylvania Dutch look are cut from folded *15" x 18" manila paper*. Draw a heart shape and cut out, leaving the two top folds intact. (See Figure 6-8.)

cut out

Figure 6-8

Color a connected, unified design of hearts, leaves, fruit, flowers, etc., in heavy *crayon*. Use bright colors. A rick-rack, wavy or straight border can be employed.

Paint over with a *black tempera paint* wash. Let dry, open and write a message on the inside of this double-heart valentine. A wash can be applied on the outside, also.

Test paint beforehand by scribbling crayon heavily on a piece of scrap manila paper. See if it "resists" the waxy crayon. If it covers the crayon, add more water to the paint.

Note: Other colors besides black may be used for the wash. Remember to omit the color used from your crayon design.

National Brotherhood Week

National Brotherhood Week is February 16–23. Programs emphasize the need for a year-round commitment to brotherhood. The sponsor is the National Conference of Christians and Jews.

In a **brotherhood art project,** students act as models, posing for each other.

Cut profiles and silhouettes of fellow students. Use *black 12" x 18" construction paper*; mount later on *white*.

Direct the children to cut directly, without pre-drawing, by looking carefully at the model.

Begin with head profile silhouettes and proceed with full-figure "action" cut-outs. Have models change positions: hands on hips; hands over head, etc. (See Figures 6-9A and 6-9B.)

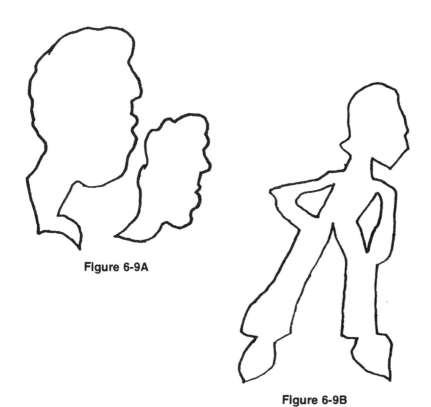

Figure 6-9A

Figure 6-9B

One approach: tell youngsters to imagine painting a thick black line around the figure; tell them to trace it in the air.

Confidence grows with practice as children see improvement after several attempts.

Follow up with a drawing lesson that also uses models. Have children look only at the outline of the model and not at the paper.

This contour approach results in sometimes funny, sometimes surprisingly realistic figures.

Create simple **stick puppets from tongue depressors.** Draw, cut and color figures depicting people of various countries. Use *stiff paper*. Paste or tape to top of depressor. (See Figure 6-10.)

Figure 6-10

Children kneel and manipulate the little puppets from behind a desk or table. They can make up original scripts for *Brotherhood Week* and perform for other classes.

Figure 6-11

The activity on **cut paper people of other lands** requires an *assortment* of *brightly colored papers*. Construct as paper dolls to be dressed, with tabs on clothing, or paste *cut paper* figures to a background. (See Figure 6-11.) Keep the shapes simple.

Groups can do research on native costumes in the library. Discuss clothes worn in different climates.

An Eskimo figure is used here as one example; hopefully, people of many nations will be represented.

Washington's Birthday

George Washington's birthday is February 22, but the legal public holiday (which is now known as "President's Day") can vary, as it is set on the third Monday in February.

Washington was the first President of the United States: "First in war, first in peace, and first in the hearts of his countrymen." Let him be the inspiration for a **Memorable Men mobile.**

Staple a rectangular *strip of heavy paper* to form a circle. Punch and add strings (four or more) according to diagram. (See Figure 6-12.)

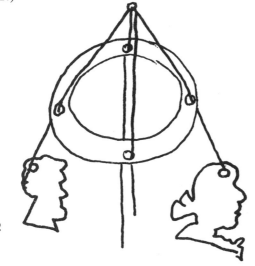

Figure 6-12

Cut *red, white, blue* or *black* profile silhouettes of George Washington in a small size from heavy paper. Punch the tops and tie to strings attached to the circle. Allow some slack for freedom of movement.

Profiles of Abraham Lincoln or other famous February figures can also be added.

Bonus Activities for February

Boy Scout Day

Boy Scouts of America Day is February 8th. It celebrates the founding of this youth organization incorporated in Washington, D. C. in 1910. It signifies the beginning of Scout Week.

"Good deed tickets" can be made from blank flash cards used in reading or math, or cut from *oaktag*.

The teacher can also make up a ditto sheet of cut-apart coupons that can be stapled into a ticket book. Cut back and front covers of *colored paper* and decorate. Tear off tickets to be redeemed one at a time.

Children can date and sign these tickets, each one promising a good deed for the lucky bearer.

For example, tickets can read: "I promise to walk the dog," or "This ticket (or coupon) good for one cleaning the basement, washing the dishes, mowing the lawn, helping my brother (sister) with his homework, taking out the trash, baby sitting, etc."

What parent wouldn't like to get one of these books for a gift!

Daniel Boone's Birthday

Daniel Boone, American frontiersman who led the way to Kentucky, was born on the 11th of February, 1734, and died in 1820.

Figure 6-13

At this time, Kentucky was part of Indian country. Indian mothers carried their babies with them. A North American Indian baby was called a **papoose**.

Cut a *9" circle* of *paper* in any color. Fold in three sides. (See Figure 6-13.)

Punch holes at top of side panels and add a *string* or *piece* of *wool*. Decorate with a crayoned Indian design. Slip in a paper "papoose." Tape it down with *clear tape* if you wish.

Purim

Purim (the Feast of Lots) is a Jewish holy day, occurring in February or March.

Purim, which began when Jews lived in Persia, honors Queen Esther. This gay holiday, a time for plays, parties and dances, celebrates the saving of Jews through the death of Haman, the king's prime minister. Wear costumes and bracelets to re-enact a Purim celebration in your classroom.

Bracelets are fun to wear and pleasing to see. Take a *1" x 8" strip* of *tag* or *cardboard* and staple into a circle to fit individual wrists loosely.

Wrap evenly with *brightly colored string* or *cord*. Change color every inch or so or make up different patterns. Be sure to tie off colors on the inside of the bracelet when you change from one to another so they do not show. (See Figure 6-14.)

Figure 6-14

Make several and wear them proudly!

Noisemakers are fun at parties.

Collect *tin cans* of different sizes.

Punch a hole with a nail or hand can opener in one end. The teacher should assist.

Put in some *beans, buttons, pebbles* or *bottle caps*. Cover the hole and outside of the can with any color *contact adhesive paper*, and apply cut-out designs in other colors.

Strings may be taped under the end contact papers for twirling the can to produce noise.

Round cardboard oatmeal boxes or the like can also be used.

Lantern Festival (End of Chinese New Year)

The Lantern Festival on February 25th in Hong Kong marks the end of Chinese New Year celebrations. Traditionally designed lanterns appear in homes, marketplaces, restaurants and temples.

Paper lanterns can be made in different sizes and papers. Try *9" x 12" poster* or *12" x 18" construction paper* in several colors. Tiny ones can serve as favors at a party.

Fold paper in half. Cut one-inch strips up from the fold to about an inch from the open top (Figure 15A.)

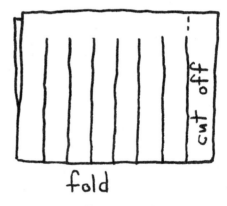

Figure 6-15A

Younger children can rule off a horizontal line at the top and the vertical lines before cutting.

Cut the last strip off completely for a handle.

Open, bring ends together and staple, tape or paste to get the lantern shape (Figure 15B.)

Figure 6-15B

Attach handle to the top on both sides.

Decorate with cut paper and hold or hang. Some lanterns might be hung from the tail of a large paper dragon!

7

HIGHLIGHTS
of the month of
MARCH

Magellan Day

Luther Burbank's Birthday

Alexander Graham Bell Patents Telephone

First Paper Money Issued in U.S.

St. Patrick's Day

Earth Day

Easter

Bird Day

Youth Art Month

Magellan Day

Magellan Day, which falls on March 6th, is sometimes called Discovery Day. In 1521 the island of Guam in the West Pacific was discovered by the explorer Ferdinand Magellan. A Portuguese navigator in the service of Spain, he also discovered the Strait of Magellan and the Philippine Islands.

Many explorers used the instrument called a compass for finding direction. Another type of compass, consisting of two pointed legs connected by a pivot, is used for drawing circles or arcs.

Stimulating an interest in design can be accomplished in many ways. One approach, to confine the shape of a design to a circle, has several possibilities for exploration. First, children practice manipulating the compass by use of wrist action.

Any size or color paper may be used. Vary the size of the circles. Some can become faces. Overlap others. Space within the circles can be broken up with a ruler. The addition of color (crayons, markers, etc.) makes the design more dynamic. Single-circle designs can also be cut out and displayed on a wall or bulletin board.

Symmetrical patterns, similar to hex signs, may be attempted. The use of a kaleidoscope as a motivational tool can produce interesting results. The circle can be folded first into several segments. Children can insert a pin in the center and spin the circle. Even a scribble design, when spun, has eye appeal.

Some multi-circle designs become **"op art"** and seem to move when you focus upon them. (See Figures 7-1A, 7-1B, and 7-1C.)

Figure 7-1A

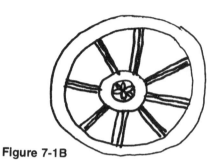

Figure 7-1B

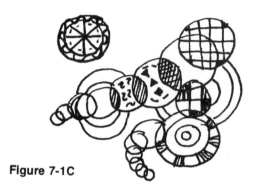

Figure 7-1C

Luther Burbank's Birthday

March 7th is the anniversary of the birth, in 1849, of Luther Burbank. He died in 1928. Burbank, an American horticulturist, developed over two hundred varieties of plants.

To make **open-up potted plant pictures** (Figure 7-2), use *white* and *light green 12" x 18" construction paper*.

Draw a large, interesting plant with stems and leaves, in a container, or cachepot. Color heavily, using any combination of browns, yellows and greens. Cut (poke scissors on line) half of pot and half of some leaves. Bend back. Paste or staple this paper (white) onto the light green background. Repeat colored pattern on back of half-bent leaves and pot, and also on light green paper to follow through the pattern so all surfaces are decorated. This creates an unusual, 3-D look to enhance your classroom for springtime.

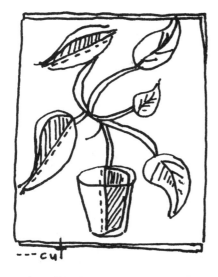

Figure 7-2

--- cut

Alexander Graham Bell Patents Telephone

Also on March 7th, in 1876, Alexander Graham Bell patented the telephone, an invention children become familiar with at an early age. Bell was born in Scotland in 1847; he died in 1922.

Inventions with a modern, sculptural flair can be tried on a small scale. Using a *block* of *scrap wood* for a base, affix nuts, bolts, screws, keys and other *small metal objects* with strong clear *glue*. (See Figure 7-3A.)

Figure 7-3A

Perhaps some preliminary pencil sketches might be in order. Move the elements around, before gluing, until the piece is pleasing from all viewpoints. Let dry. *Spray paint* (black, silver, gold), either flat (matte) or glossy enamel, finishes the construction. Use spray paint in a well-ventilated room. Place the inventions in a cardboard carton with one side cut out before spraying.

What function, if any, do these inventions convey? Discuss individual ideas. Allow the collective imagination of the class to make these decisions or conclusions.

All-wood sculptures could be attempted for another lesson. Reproductions of the larger structures of the artist Louise Nevelson might serve as inspiration to older students.

These pieces can be presented to parents and friends as gifts to be displayed in the home. They are unique conversation pieces! Other "invention" designs can be boldly created using *wide-line black markers* on *large white paper*. Look at and discuss facets of mechanical items, such as a can opener, hair dryer, toaster, garlic press, etc. Draw an invention in the center of the paper. Follow through with lines and curves borrowed from the center drawing until paper is covered (Figure 7-3B). In other words, extend patterns to edge. Rulers may be used if a more disciplined approach is desired.

Figure 7-3B

First Paper Money Issued in U.S.

On March 10th, in 1862, the first paper money was issued in the United States. Children are accustomed to handling this medium of exchange. Transactions take place daily when they go to the store, or bring money to school.

Play dollars used in games can be brought in for an activity based on **currency**. Different denominations of paper money can be discussed in terms of design, famous people, etc.

Children can then design, draw and color their own bills, creating unique denominations, and honoring people of their own choosing. A humorous approach using cartoon characters for "funny money" may be employed. Coin rubbings (see June chapter) may be done also.

Since the tie-in to math is a natural one, some children could create a play store from a large carton. Slit or cut away the back so children can "enter." Cut out a window from the front, add a cardboard or wooden shelf with boxes of different products, and decorate with paint or cut-out pictures of foods. Add a sign, and "business" can begin.

St. Patrick's Day

St. Patrick's Day, March 17th, commemorates Bishop Patrick, the patron saint of Ireland. In 432 A.D. he left Severn Valley in England and introduced Christianity to Ireland.

Today, remembrances include interesting legends, shamrocks, parades, and "the wearing of the green."

Leprechauns are made of paper, in two shades of green. They can be "mini" or "maxi." Touches of white (eyes, pipe) may be added.

The basic shape is a cylinder, created from a stapled rectangle. Add strips for arms and legs, a head and a hat, and boots and hands—all of cut paper. Trim with pipe, bow tie, shamrock eyes and buttons, etc. (See Figure 7-4.)

Children with Irish or English heritages can contribute favorite family recipes for a **class recipe book,** which, when completed, can be "dittoed" or printed, and sold by the school or given as gifts.

Parents can cooperate by sending in a favorite recipe, preferably checked first for accuracy.

Often, varying ethnic groups are represented, and recipes will be diverse in origin. Children investigate and research several cookbooks. Some recipes might be tried out as a classroom project under teacher or parent supervision. A trip to a restaurant would be a valuable motivating or culminating activity!

Covers for recipe books could depict people from different nations, or portions of maps of the countries or areas represented. Pictures of food or names of the dishes in other languages could be incorporated into both the cover design and the inside pages.

A large map of the world can be reproduced on mural paper by using an opaque projector. Strings, ribbons or marker lines can be added to show homelands of parents and grandparents of students. Small flags of these countries can be added.

This project can be done on a smaller scale, using individual printed maps available in most schools. A color key can be added, thus reinforcing skills in map reading.

Individual continents can be drawn and cut out. If pasted on

Figure 7-4

light cardboard and cut into pieces, puzzles can be constructed, or mobiles created.

Papier mâché globes, with balloon centers, can be painted and coded in the same way.

Earth Day

Earth Day falls on the 21st, as does the spring equinox. Programs to replenish the earth often open this season. Due to the dwindling of the earth's natural resources, there has been much publicity about ecology and the environment, and many ideas have come to the fore regarding this world-wide problem.

Young children especially seem to enjoy making **pinwheel flowers**. They can be large or small, depending on the size of the square of paper used. Bright spring colors are appropriate. Demonstrate the cutting on the diagonal from all four corners (Figure 7-5A).

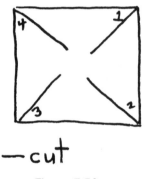

— cut

Figure 7-5A

Overlap all right-hand corners and affix to center with a *paper fastener*.

For a stem, fold a long strip of paper twice (for strength) and push the brad through. Staple on paper leaves, or twist on leaves of tissue paper.

If 12″ x 18″ paper is used, bend left corner down to form a square. Cut off for pinwheel (flower) part. Cut remaining piece in half. Use one piece for stem (fold twice lengthwise), the other for cutting leaves.

A paper flower pot may also be added. Fold edges in twice for a 3-D bulletin board display. (See Figure 7-5B.)

Figure 7-5B

Fantasy insects, concocted of *egg carton sections* and *pipe cleaners,* add a sprightly note to any classroom.

Cut sections apart with scissors or narrow-blade knife, according to sizes desired. Paint with gay dots or other designs, and link together with colored pipe cleaners or florist wire. A paper punch and a stapler can aid in fastening sections.

Add glued-on buttons for eyes and braided or "fluffed" wool for a tail. Pipe cleaners also serve as antennae. (See Figure 7-6.)

Figure 7-6

Plastic-coated egg cartons in pastel colors can be left as is or spray painted. If tempera paint is used, mix with some detergent to aid adhesion.

Giant paper strip flowers (Figure 7-7) add cheer to classroom decor. Cut several strips on the paper cutter about an inch wide and

Figure 7-7

18 inches long for each child. Use *bright colors*: yellow, orange, light green, dark green.

If children work in groups, staplers can be shared, and no tedious pasting will be required.

To begin, staple a small circle (or twist one strip to get a "circle within a circle") and add on several daisy-like petals all around it. Petals are simply strips bent or looped in half.

A straight strip(s) is the stem. A wavy, free-form stem, cut from a long piece of paper, could be used also.

Add several groups of bent (looped) smaller strips for leaves. Smaller circles or zig-zag patterns can be made from rolled sections of strips and stapled inside the leaves for detail and interest.

Punch, add a string and hang from the lights, or make one wall a garden.

Figure 7-8

Paper roll magazine flowerpots (Figure 7-8) may not be waterproof, but they certainly can add a decorative note to a shelf or table.

Cut several one-inch wide magazine strips on the paper cutter for each child. Paste end to end and roll up tightly into a disk. Put fingers in the center and gently press outward until form extends into a small flowerpot shape. Size depends on size of disk, or number of strips used. Larger bowls can be made, too. Just keep adding on strips (paste) until disk is size desired.

If magazine colors and print are satisfying to the eye, the pot can be unpainted. Spray paint in any color is easy to apply, and covers inside and outside quickly. Before painting, white glue, thinned with water, can be applied all over to seal surfaces and prevent disk from coming apart.

When dry, the pot may be weighted with plaster and artificial flowers inserted before plaster sets.

Commercial disks in varying sizes, similar to cash register tapes, may also be purchased.

Easter

Easter may occur in March. Easter Sunday is celebrated in late March or in April.

Good Friday is a solemn day, while Easter Sunday is one of the most joyous. Many popular customs and beliefs are connected with Easter. The giving of eggs can be traced back to ancient times, when the egg was an emblem of the universe.

Young children enjoy making **"Chicken-in-an-Egg."** Cut a large oval, freehand or on the fold, from *white 12" x 18" construction paper*. Explain that an egg is wider at one end, and narrows at the other end to a rounded point.

Cut an uneven, jagged slit across the egg shape by poking with scissors. (See Figure 7-9A.)

Draw a simple chick shape on *yellow paper*. Color beak and eye, and make small "v" or "u" shapes with brown crayon to suggest feathers. If cotton or cotton batting is available, apply paste to paper and cover chick's body with a light layer on both sides, leaving feet, beak and eye exposed.

Insert into slit in egg, taping on back of egg to secure. Chick can also be stapled in place. (See Figure 7-9B.)

Figure 7-9A

Figure 7-9B

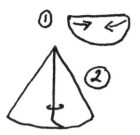

Figure 7-10A

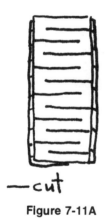

Figure 7-10B

Cone bunnies can be made tiny, medium-sized, or large. Some children might want to create a whole family. Make the cone by drawing a half-circle, utilizing the edge of paper as the base. Cut out, and form the cone by overlapping the straight edges. Trim, if necessary, so cone "sits" properly. (See Figure 7-10A.) Add (paste) a "combination" head and ears. Decorate, before pasting, with features and whiskers. Be sure to place head high enough on cone. (See Figure 7-10B.) Paste on a small wad of cotton or tissue paper in back for a tail.

Super Bunny makes a big hit as an Easter ornament.

Fold (short way) *12" x 18" white construction paper* twice (into fourths). Fold the last (open) strip back. Make scissor cuts evenly on alternate sides, about a half-inch apart. (See Figure 7-11A.) Open the paper to original size—carefully.

Pull gently, to stretch or expand the paper. Add (staple or paste) a paper rabbit head, ears and four paws. (See Figure 7-11B.) On any lower back strip, add a wad of colored tissue paper or cotton for a tail.

Punch a hole in top of head, add string, and hang. It bounces merrily!

—cut

Figure 7-11A

Figure 7-11B

Bonus Activities for March

Bird Day

March 21st is Bird Day in Iowa. Some states combine Bird Day and Arbor Day with Luther Burbank's birthday on the 7th. Others celebrate it early in May.

At times, Bird Day is arranged in connection with the Audubon Societies, whose purpose is to preserve and protect the country's wild birds.

First celebrated in 1894 by the schools of Oil City, Pennsylvania, its observance is sponsored by the U.S. Department of Agriculture. The governor of each state usually announces the date through proclamation.

Children can make **Bird Day drawings** of birds of their choice. Observation of local birds becomes natural motivation. Pictures in books and magazines can also be used for reference. Refined, small drawings on sturdy paper should be colored on both sides. Punch, string, and let hang down from center of "Expanded Spheres." (See May chapter, "Memorial Day," on the making of patriotic *spheres*, and follow directions.)

Paper strip owls (Figure 7-12) can be pasted, but stapling is faster and less frustrating.

Cut several one-inch strips of *black construction paper, 12" x 18"* wide. Cut 18 inches long; cut some in half. Begin with a

Figure 7-12

circle. Roll smaller circles, and circles within circles, to create large eyes. Add straight, small, triangular pieces for ears; longer, fringed end strips for added interest. The nose is a small piece, cut to a "beak" shape; the claws are folded, narrow strips. Punch and string, to hang.

The owl takes shape quickly; variations are, of course, most welcome.

Youth Art Month

March is Youth Art Month. Sponsored by the Crayon, Water Color and Craft Institute of Newtown, Connecticut, its purpose is to promote the importance and value of art participation in the development of children.

Contour line creations seem to fascinate children when displayed. They often take on the quality of "op art" by appearing to ripple and move.

If *crayons* or a similar medium are used, colors can be varied, repeated, or a color scheme can be utilized. *Black markers* alone create impressive pictures, too.

Choose any small, simple, recognizable outline drawing (a flower, figure, etc.) and draw in the center of *15" x 18"* (or larger) *manila paper*.

Continue following the outline shape (lines not touching at any point) to the edges of the paper. (See Figure 7-13.)

Figure 7-13

A project on **rhythm and variety of line design** (Figure 7-14) requires cutting irregular (jagged, wavy, etc.) strips of paper, and mounting on same size background paper. 12″ x 18″ paper is adequate. Leave a space between each piece. Children should be careful not to flip pieces over. Strips should be arranged before pasting. All strips will not be used because of spaces left between them.

A small fish, sun, boat, etc. can be added at the top for interest.

Any colors can be employed, and all results will differ. *Blue* or *black* paper on *white* is effective.

Figure 7-14

8

HIGHLIGHTS
of the month of
APRIL

April Fools' Day

Pony Express Postal Service Began

Army Day

Commodore Perry Day

National Library Week

Pan-American Day

Leonardo da Vinci's Birthday

Paul Revere's Ride

Arbor Day

John James Audubon's Birthday

National Laugh Week

Lee Surrenders to Grant

Circus Comes to Town

Dinosaurs (Bones First Recognized)

Walpurgis Night (Witches' Sabbath)

April Fools' Day

April Fools', or All Fools' day, is the first day of the month. It probably began with pranks played due to the confusion that resulted from the adoption of a new calendar in France in 1564.

Although it is not an official holiday recognized by government or encouraged by schools, we can enjoy playing jokes on others and expect to fall prey to them ourselves on this day.

Optical illusions can lead to experimentation in art. For an interesting trick of vision involving color, have students draw and color a *green* heart, border it in *yellow*, and place a *black* dot in the center of the heart. (See Figure 8-1.)

Figure 8-1

Stare at the dot for about twenty seconds. Then look at a blank white wall.

Children will be surprised to see an afterimage of a *red* heart with a *blue* border. They can experiment with different shapes and color combinations.

For example, an orange heart bordered in purple, with a black dot in its center, is perceived as a light yellow heart with a light blue center.

Older children can do research into this visual phenomenon, investigating the "whys."

Folded *white paper, 12" x 18", 6" x 9"*, etc., can be used in the following manner. Draw the heart or other shape on the bottom half, stare at the dot, then glance at the upper blank white half of the paper.

Children find this a simple but exciting activity in altered perception.

Silly Simple Strip People are made from rectangles of *white paper* in varying sizes. Small or large, three or more can be pasted onto a *colored paper background* for added emphasis.

Cut each rectangle as shown in Figure 8-2A. Roll the middle strip down, for the face, and paste. Do not press flat, if a dimensional look is desired. Bend the hands/arms of one rectangle; leave another with arms up. Vary the positions further by bending one knee (one of bottom strips), etc.

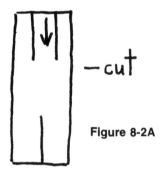

Figure 8-2A

Hands and feet (or fingers and toes) can be cut with a few strokes of a scissors.

Add features and any other touches with a *fine-line marker*. Try for a comical flair. (See Figure 8-2B.)

Children of all ages can have fun with this project. The degree of sophistication achieved depends on the age and ability of each child.

Figure 8-2B

Pony Express Postal Service Began

On the 3rd of April, 1860, the Pony Express Postal Service began. The system of carrying and delivering mail by riders on swift ponies operated from April, 1860, to October, 1861, between St. Joseph, Missouri and Sacramento, California.

The Pony Express can inspire an art project featuring **repetitive design**.

Photographs, paintings and pictures of horses can be brought in by the teacher for study. Libraries will yield others. Discussions of

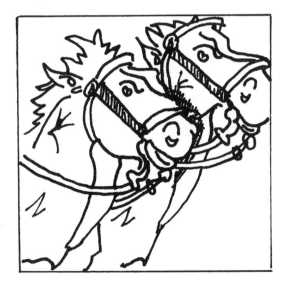

Figure 8-3

animals in motion and in repose will help. Sports pages in newspapers and magazines can serve as motivational aids.

Several good pencil sketches might result from a trip to the zoo or circus.

Heads of horses can be incorporated into pictures emphasizing repetitive design. (See Figure 8-3.)

Some children might try sketching smaller animals, such as rabbits, cats, or dogs, from life.

Original paintings might be the end result of these explorations.

Army Day

In 1935, by action of the Senate, April 6th was named as the holiday called Army Day. It had, however, been observed unofficially for many years.

Several dramatic reproductions of peace posters are available for motivation in an activity on **poster making**.

Use simple shapes and any letter-cutting procedure—block to free form.

Stress some basics of poster-making. Posters should be eye-catching, clear, and convey a message. Avoid small details.

Unity can be achieved by the use of one or two striking colors rather than many colors.

For one cut paper example, see Figure 8-4.

Figure 8-4

Commodore Perry Day

April 10th is designated as Commodore Perry Day. Matthew Calbraith Perry, Commodore in the U.S. Navy, was the negotiator of the first treaty between the United States and Japan, on March 31, 1854. He was born April 10, 1794 and died March 4, 1858.

Easy origami projects are based on an art form of that name, which originated in Japan.

A paper house(s) is made from a square of any color *flexible paper*. Fold twice one way; twice the other. Cut on lines as in Figure 8-5A.

Fold in, on cut sides, until roof and sides are formed. Paste or staple together. (See Figure 8-5B.)

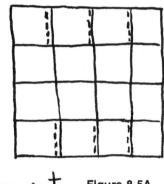

--- cut   **Figure 8-5A**   **Figure 8-5B**

Cut out windows and doors or paste on small squares.

Make several houses, in different sizes, and staple on for additions, such as a porch or garage.

Add a chimney by folding a small rectangle twice, and pasting. Cut a hole in the roof, and insert, or slit bottom of chimney, bend, and paste down.

For a second project, create a whale from light paper—any size square.

Fold across, on the diagonal, for a triangle (Figure 8-5C).

Fold down on both sides; keep even with the folded edge of the triangle (Figure 8-5D).

Fold the two edges up (on both sides) for fins (Figure 8-5E).

Press in to form flat nose (Figure 8-5F).

Fold back (end in and up) to form tail (Figure 8-5G).

Slit (cut with scissors) ends of tail and bend opposite ways. Add eye and mouth detail with marker or crayon (Figure 8-5H).

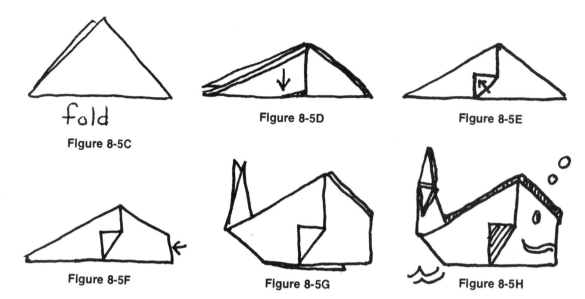

fold

Figure 8-5C

Figure 8-5D

Figure 8-5E

Figure 8-5F

Figure 8-5G

Figure 8-5H

Origami hat, boat, star and airplane are described in other lessons.

National Library Week

National Library Week, April 13–19, has as its purpose the goal of creating a better-read, better-informed America. The National Book Committee, along with the American Library Association of New York, encourages life-time reading habits and greater use of the public libraries.

Descriptive word pictures combine art and language.

Children will enjoy trying to think up more and more words, once they begin.

Use any word, and attempt to depict its meaning by the way it is written. Add a few lines or pictorial elements, if necessary. (See Figure 8-6.)

Naturally, some words lend themselves to this activity more readily than others.

For slow starters, list some words on the chalkboard, like "little," "big," "thin," "dive," "wide," "up," "stretch," "fall."

Box scenes of favorite stories reinforce the concepts of background, foreground and middleground.

Having children bring in boxes of all sizes, with lids, if possi-

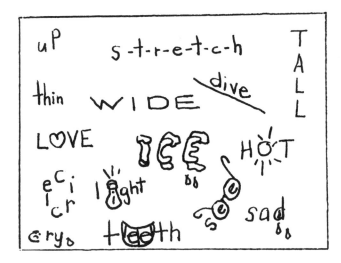

Figure 8-6

ble. Cut out the inside of a shoebox lid, leaving sides for a frame, and staple a piece of plastic wrap or acetate on the inside.

Mini-scenes can be made from tiny boxes; giant ones from large crates or cartons.

Figures of paper can be suspended by using thread and clear tape, for stories like *Peter Pan*, etc.

On any figures meant to stand, leave a tab at the bottom, fold, and paste down. Figures can be pasted to light cardboard, for body.

Outside of box(es) can be painted or cover with colored papers, wallpaper, etc.

Boxes can be decorated to resemble T.V. sets, with antennas, knobs, etc.

Children can also utilize miniature objects of all kinds in their scenes.

For **"marbleized" book jackets**, you will need a large old plastic *tub* or metal *basin,* and *enamel paint* in several colors.

Half fill with water. Drip in a few colors with a spoon, and stir gently with a stick or straw.

Lay on a piece of paper (bond, construction, etc.) for a few seconds and lift carefully. Let dry. Fold into jacket as described in November lesson on "Blot Painting Book Covers."

Add more paint as it is needed.

Results are accidental, but dramatic.

This idea can be used in several ways. On holidays, pre-cut a heart, rabbit, shamrock, etc., and dip in appropriate colors.

Pieces of Masonite with these interesting "crazes" can be framed as paintings, and make exciting gifts.

No diagram can do justice to the results!

Pan-American Day

Pan-American Day is April 14th by Presidential proclamation, issued for this day each year.

This holiday belongs to two great continents—the Americas. The United States, Mexico, and the Republics of Central and South America observe it in the spirit of international loyalty.

National flags are displayed and ceremonies are held that contribute to world peace and understanding of our sister nations.

To make **Pan-American maps**, shapes of the two continents and countries within can be traced or copied from large classroom maps, ditto maps, or geography and social studies books.

Spread areas to be covered with mucilage. Use a thin brush.

Have colored salts ready. Prepare beforehand by rubbing table *salt* with *colored chalks* in small packets made from *waxed paper*.

Sprinkle salt, one area at a time, onto the map. Shake off the excess before going on to the next section.

Be sure to include a key for these maps.

Leonardo da Vinci's Birthday

Leonardo da Vinci, born on the 15th of April, was an Italian artist and inventor (1452–1519). He left a rich legacy, both in the scientific and the artistic realms.

Designer of the first armored tank and the magnetic needle compass, he also built the first airplane.

He achieved immortality through the creation of two of the most popular masterpieces in history, the *Last Supper* and the *Mona Lisa*.

A **clothesline art show** (indoors or out) offers both students and teachers an opportunity to see works created by others in all grades displayed in one place.

Invention drawings should definitely be included, if the show is to honor da Vinci! (See March chapter: "Magic Marker Invention Design.")

All art work, mounted or unmounted, can be attached easily

with clothespins. The line can be strung up in the classroom, halls, or outside between two trees.

Work should be labeled and signed, so young artists can experience the pride of recognition.

Parents and friends can be invited.

Three-dimensional work can be displayed on tables, and demonstrations can be held at scheduled times.

Paul Revere's Ride

On the 18th of April in 1775, Paul Revere, a Boston patriot, rode through the streets to warn the Minutemen that the redcoats were coming. The English soldiers who were on their way to Concord, Massachusetts, to seize the ammunition stored there were thwarted.

Use brown or other *mural paper* for a group-inspired effort utilizing **mixed media.** Paul Revere's ride can be re-created with *tempera paint, oil crayons, pastels, colored chalk, water crayons, cut paper,* etc.

Students can work alone or in groups on their own interpretations of this famous event. (See Figure 8-7.)

Figure 8-7

Differing approaches and aspects of this historic happening, together with application of varied media, will create an unusual mural.

National Arbor Day

National Arbor Day is celebrated on the 25th. Its purpose is to encourage protection, planting and appreciation of forest and shade trees. The first observance in the United States was in Nebraska, on April 10, in 1872. Arbor Day is observed on the last Friday in April in some states.

"Arbor" is the Latin word for "tree." Many trees are planted as memorials, and there is an old Aztec custom of planting a tree when a child is born.

To make **Arbor Day trees**, get a large bag(s) of *popcorn* and have the children collect several light *branches*, with twigs, suitable for pasting to a paper background.

Rubber cement or *white glue* can serve as an adhesive for both the popcorn and twigs. (See Figure 8-8.)

Figure 8-8

Use *colored chalk* to add interest to the centers of the popcorn "blossoms."

A **wishing well planter** makes a pleasing gift. Collect snap-apart *clothespins* and *baby food jars*. Take clothespins apart and use singly. Glue together, with *white glue*, around the jar.

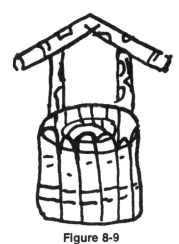

Figure 8-9

Add four halves for sides and top (hold until glue sets) to form top of wishing well. (See Figure 8-9.)

Stain or shellac. Add soil and a small seedling.

John James Audubon's Birthday

John James Audubon (1785–1851) was an American ornithologist and artist. His birthdate was the 26th of April. He recorded the wild birds of 19th century America in watercolor.

The name of America's most famous naturalist is well known through the efforts of the National Association of Audubon Societies, which attempts to preserve and protect our country's wild birds.

To make **wild bird pictures**, tear *colored paper* into small (not tiny) sized, irregular pieces. Fill in a pre-drawn bird shape by overlapping. (See Figure 8-10.)

Figure 8-10

Older children can elaborate on this idea by adding greater detail or making a composition of several birds.

Spaces between straight-edged, geometric pieces can be left to simulate "grout," for another approach. Cut, do not tear, the shapes.

Colored magazine pages create yet another effect.

Bonus Activities for April

National Laugh Week

The purpose of National Laugh Week, April 1–8, is to promote a national sense of humor and happiness. Its sponsor is Humor Societies of America in New York.

April Fools' Day is certainly a good time to begin this week of fun.

An **open-mouth paper puppet head** is a versatile activity. Inverted, it can also serve as a candy dish at a party!

Begin with a *12" square* (or smaller) of any color *construction paper*. Fold one way, then the other, and open.

Fold in all four points to center. Turn paper over. Fold in all points to center on this side also.

Re-crease folds by pressing, both horizontally and vertically, to increase flexibility.

Turn paper over. Insert fingers, one into each pocket, and press, bringing fingers together.

Manipulate fingers so that the shape opens and closes. (See Figures 8-11A, 8-11B, and 8-11C.)

Figure 8-11A

Figure 8-11B

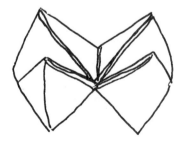

Figure 8-11C

Some children like to add a simple paper body, cut on the fold, and stapled to the head. (See Figure 8-11D.)

Figure 8-11D

Students can create their own characters, write their own humorous scripts, and put on a show!

Lee Surrenders to Grant

On the 9th of April, 1865, General Lee surrendered the Confederate Army to Union General Grant.

The Civil War was fought between the North and the South in the United States from 1861–1865.

Blue and gray were the colors of the opposing factions. For **op art paper weaving**, cut 12″ strips of one color unevenly: wavy, zig-zag, thin, wide, etc.

Use *12″ x 18″ paper*. Fold a sheet in half, and cut strips for the loom, up from the fold, to within one inch of the open end. Cut these unevenly also. (See Figures 8-12A, 8-12B, and 8-12C.)

Weave the strips through, in and out, pushing them together as close as possible. Paste the ends down.

If weaving strips are cut longer, edges can be cut and fringed.

18″ x 24″ or 24″ x 36″ paper makes larger, more impressive "woven" pictures.

Display together, without spaces between them, on a large bulletin board.

—cut

Figure 8-12A

fold

Figure 8-12B

Figure 8-12C

They can be viewed as is, or utilized as an interesting background for cut paper silhouettes (in another color) depicting heroes or scenes of the Civil War.

Circus Comes to Town

April is the beginning of circus season, since many circuses, large and small, begin their tours now. Ringling Brothers-Barnum and Bailey, the biggest circus, opens in New York City and starts across the country.

Cylinder clowns can be constructed in small or large versions.

Sturdy, large, flexible *colored paper* is stapled or taped into a standing cylinder. Build from this base.

Add a large strip, attached at the back, for arms. Add large, cut paper gloves.

For feet, a large heart shape, flattened and folded at the tip, is stapled to the bottom.

Head, hat and ruff are stapled at the top. Put a flower in the clown's hands. (See Figure 8-13.)

These classroom friends will enliven the atmosphere.

Markers are good for other details, such as buttons, etc.

Figure 8-13

A **paper animal train** adds to the circus feeling.

Cut several vertical rectangles from *9" x 12"* or *12" x 18" paper* in bright colors. Add paper circles for wheels. (See Figure 8-14A.)

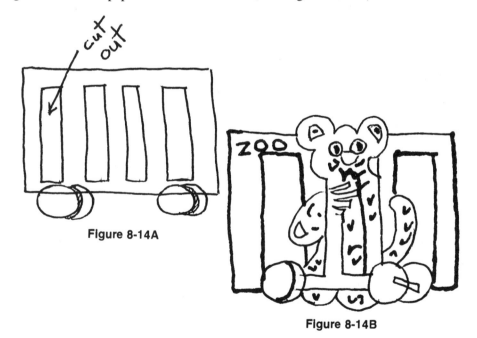

Figure 8-14A

Figure 8-14B

Construct zoo or circus animals from simple geometric shapes. Insert into "bars" of "cages." (See Figure 8-14B.)

Attach individual cages with small straight strips by stapling or pasting together.

These, too, like the clowns, can be made larger, or used for scenery.

Dinosaurs (Bones First Recognized)

In the late 1700's, dinosaur bones were first recognized in Europe and the United States. Artists' renderings in spring-like settings suggested a possible April date.

Dinosaurs lived on this earth 200 million years ago. When the climate changed from warm to cool, and different plants began to grow, the cold-blooded creatures eventually disappeared.

Have children collect bones from their mothers' kitchens or from a cooperative butcher—chicken, marrow, steak, and other bones. The bones should be boiled or washed thoroughly before being brought into the classroom, where they are stored in plastic bags until there are enough for **bones and glue sculpture**.

Bones can be drilled, sanded, shellacked or painted (enamel). *Wire* and/or *white* or other *strong glue* are used for constructing animals and abstract designs.

Results can be glued to *blocks* of *wood*.

Details can be added. Leather, raffia, or felt scraps can be employed for finishing touches.

Walpurgis Night (Witches' Sabbath)

In northern Europe, April 30th is known as Walpurgis Night. St. Walpurgis was an early missionary to Germany; she was born in England in the eighth century.

Walpurgis Night, celebrated mostly by university students, is also called "Witches' Sabbath" and "Eve of May Day." On this night, fires are kindled to burn out the witches.

Striking silhouettes of a **witch's hat and hair** are made in traditional *black* and *orange* colors. *12" x 18" construction paper* is suitable.

Choose one color for witch, one for background.

Draw lightly, in pencil, a side view of an ugly witch: big nose, warts, and hat.

Cut out and paste or staple onto the background color.

Children can cut out some simple shapes from the witch's head (before pasting), such as a circle for the eye, etc. Stress the fact that it should be large, scary, simple, recognizable. (See Figure 8-15.)

Older children might attempt full-figure witch silhouettes, complete with cat and broom.

Figure 8-15

9

HIGHLIGHTS
of the month of
MAY

May Day

Be Kind to Animals Month (Humane Sunday)

Apple Blossom Festival (Pa. and Va.)

Children's Day (Japan)

Mother's Day

Holland Tulip Time Festival

Buddha's Birthday

National Maritime Day

African Freedom Day

Memorial Day

Festival of Weeks (Shabuoth)

Birthday of First Postage Stamp

Captain Kidd Tried for Piracy

Ben Franklin Invents Bifocals

Indians Sell Manhattan to Peter Minuit

May Day

May Day customs and festivals stem from ancient Rome. Flowery celebrations, with flowers, baskets, wreaths and garlands, marked spring's beginning and signified good luck for the coming year.

May baskets can be hung on classroom or neighbors' doors, and filled with small flowers: real, artificial, dried or paper.

To celebrate May 1st, a simple cone basket can be constructed from a *paper half-circle*. Draw a half-circle on a piece of rectangular paper and cut out. Holding the half-circle with the flat end up, overlap edges and staple, or paste into a conical shape. Add a paper strip handle, and decorate. (See Figures 9-1A, 9-1B, and 9-1C.)

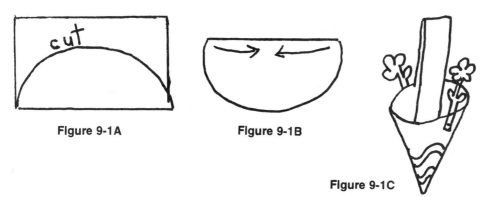

Figure 9-1A   Figure 9-1B

Figure 9-1C

Another kind of basket can be made from any size paper strip, preferably *stiff* paper. Staple to form a circle. Add a handle and a bottom. Flowers are drawn directly on the strip, and the excess paper cut away. (See Figures 9-2A and 9-2B.)

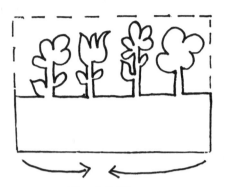

Figure 9-2A

Figure 9-2B

Figure 9-3

A second interesting project for this day is a **plastic lid floral mobile.** It can be hung in school or at home.

Three or more *plastic lid covers*, from coffee cans or the like, are punched and strung together with *wool* or *string*. They can be spray painted. *Pictures* of *flowers*, either drawn or cut from magazines, are pasted inside each lid. *Ribbons* and *glitter* may be added for gaiety and originality. (See Figure 9-3.)

Be Kind to Animals Month (Humane Sunday)

May is Be Kind to Animals Month. Humane Sunday falls on the first Sunday. During this time, children can be made aware of the importance of projects promoting animal welfare, prevention of cruelty to animals, and the nature of animal protective agencies.

Many children have pets; others are exposed to the care and feeding of rabbits, hamsters and guinea pigs in the classroom setting.

Using this natural inspiration, the teacher can easily incorporate the following projects into lessons relating to animals. Trips to local zoos and animal habitats add zest and motivation!

One idea, **paper scored animals**, employs the paper sculpture technique of scoring. With some practice, children can deviate from this suggested activity and experiment with creating several kinds of animals, both real and fanciful.

Begin with a rectangular piece of paper (construction paper or a stiffer grade); size depends on size desired (e.g., 6″ x 9″; 9″ x 12″). Fold, draw half of animal, and cut out. (See Figure 9-4A.) Open and score all broken lines on both sides of animal. To score, hold scissors, open, by laying in palm of hand, and go over the lines by pressing with a firm, continuous movement. Use the sharper scissor blade. Do not press so hard that paper is cut through.

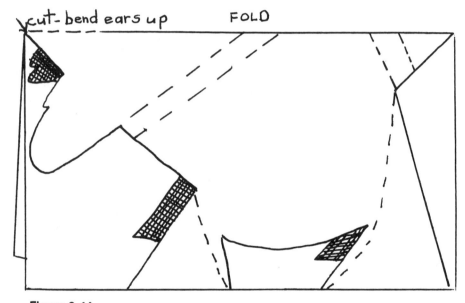

Figure 9-4A

Perhaps scoring should be practiced first on scrap paper, until children feel comfortable and confident. Scoring "grooves" the paper, making it easier to flex, thus allowing the animal to stand. Press on scored lines until head, tail and neck "pop up" easily. Decorate, adding eyes, fringed mane, etc., with *crayons* and/or *cut paper*. (See Figure 9-4B.) Stand completed animals on window sill, or use in box scenes, and enjoy!

Figure 9-4B

Fringed paper animals, made by curling small pieces of cut paper with scissors, add an interesting dimensional effect to flat paper pictures. Any color combination can be used.

For a cat, cut a *circle of paper* containing two triangular ears, an *oval* for the body (with a long tail), and *four* simple *shapes* for paws. (See Figure 9-5A.)

Figure 9-5A

Note: To save time in any project when more than one of the same shape is desired, either fold the paper, or place the number of pieces desired in one pile before drawing and cutting. This saves time and effort.

If you choose to mount the animal, paste on a *contrasting color background*.

Next, cut several *small rectangles*. Snip, making long scissor cuts, and curl with scissor blade, or by wrapping around a pencil. Paste on the animal so curled edges stock up (Figure 9-5B). Add cut paper eyes, nose and whiskers. Make dogs, etc., by using other simple basic shapes and covering them with curled rectangles in the same manner. Brown, black and white paper can be combined to create a pleasing Schnauzer! (See Figure 9-5C.)

Figure 9-5B

Figure 9-5C

Papier mâché newspaper animals can be made from any traditional papier mâché recipe (soaking *newspaper strips* in a bucket of watered-down *wheat* or *wallpaper paste*), or from *manufactured prepared rolls* of bandage-like material containing plaster of Paris. The latter simply requires cutting off the desired length, dipping in water, and applying. Directions come with the product. Drying time is much faster, and one layer is usually sufficient to cover the newspaper base.

Wad one half of a large sheet of newspaper for the head. Tell the children to crush it into a ball, as if they intended to throw it away! Two or more wadded up balls (depending on length of body desired) are then wrapped inside another, larger newspaper sheet for the body. Two rolled newspaper strips (make them sturdy) are added for legs. (See Figure 9-6A.) Loosely join parts together with masking tape, adding tail and ears, also of smaller pieces of crushed newspaper. Animals can be designed to sit or stand. (See Figure 9-6B.) Cover with several layers of mâché and let dry for a few days. If Plastercraft materials are used, no final layer of paper toweling is necessary.

Figure 9-6A

Figure 9-6B

Paint with *tempera* or *acrylic*.

What a special gift for a younger sister or brother!

Apple Blossom Festival (Pa. and Va.)

The Apple Blossom Festival, annual springtime event in Pennsylvania and Virginia, affords an opportunity to introduce children to the art of **"subtractive" sculpture**. If *apples* are used, the head sculpture is formed by cutting away, or reducing, rather than "adding on" pieces.

Directions are easy. After studying the hollows of your face in a mirror, or thinking about an imaginary creature, simply bite or cut away portions of any whole apple. Use of any knife by a child requires close supervision and instruction.

As in any sculptural project, turn the apple so you can see how it looks from all sides.

When finished, put the apple in a *container* (plastic or glass) of *lemon juice* for approximately ten minutes. Plastic "squeeze" bottles of lemon juice are most convenient for this purpose. Remove apple. Add *thumb tacks, buttons,* or other objects for eyes and teeth, or other desired effects. (See Figure 9-7.)

Figure 9-7

Let dry for a few days in a dry place. The apple will shrink considerably in size and wrinkle in a fascinating way.

Display and enjoy your wizened creatures. You might even use them for puppet heads! Coat head with Polymer Gloss Medium or white glue thinned with water. Paint lips and eyes with acrylics, if desired.

To dress an apple head doll, staple a sturdy piece of *cardboard* into an appropriate size cone. Push a small stick (a cotton swab stick minus the cotton works well) into the bottom of the apple. Insert into cone. If head is wobbly, secure with a small strip of plasticine clay. Glue on cotton or cotton batting for hair.

Use scrap material to dress; pin or staple onto cone. Add a dress, scarf, bandana, apron, etc. Arms can be a flexible strip of cardboard covered with material, and pinned into place.

Hands can also be pieces of dried apple. Insert a small bunch of artificial flowers.

Bottle caps or toy straw hats look good, too.

Children's Day (Japan)

Children's Day, May 5th, is a national holiday in Japan. It is a relatively new holiday, begun in 1922, after the modern calendar had been approved. Children's Day is now being celebrated here, too.

All children enjoy the activities of kite-making and kite-flying.

Colorful paper fish, Oriental in feeling, can be made from large sheets of *tissue paper*. If a pattern is desired, use *large manila paper*, sketch a simple fish outline, and cut out. Trace on tissue paper (two sheets) and cut out both. A light color, like yellow, is best. Paste edges together, leaving mouth open. Stuff to desired thickness with assorted bright colors of crumpled scraps of tissue paper. Paste edges of mouth to close. Add curled tissue scraps for fins, and add an eye on both sides of fish. (See Figure 9-8.)

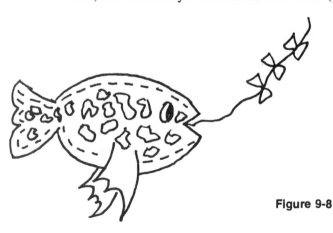

Figure 9-8

Make several, if the spirit moves you. Add *strings* and *ribbons* and fly your kite. They also look well if hung from the ceiling in your classroom. The transparent tissue allows inside colors to show through.

Mother's Day

Mother's Day, by Presidential proclamation, is observed annually on the second Sunday in May. Gifts and cards are traditional. It is helpful to offer the suggestion that a sister, favorite aunt, or grandmother can also be honored.

For a **tissue paper flower card**, pre-cut tissue paper into rectangles (size depends on size desired). 4½" x 9½" is a good size for a card.

Shades of one color (purple, pink, etc.) are particularly attractive. Six rectangles, neatly stacked, are needed for each flower. Cut edges off after fan-folding the stack. Tie in the middle (not tightly) with string. (See Figure 9-9A.)

Gently pull each layer towards you, one at a time, until all six pieces are forward. Turn and pull layers on other side in the same way until flower is completed. (See Figure 9-9B.)

Figure 9-9A

Figure 9-9B

Figure 9-9C

Add leaves and stem, of *green tissue, soft poster,* or *construction paper. Florist wire* or a *green pipe cleaner* could also serve as the stem. Twist tissue leaves on at varying places. Staple or paste to front of white folded paper. (See Figure 9-9C.)

Write an appropriate greeting inside.

An interesting and utilitarian gift of **make-believe milk glass** can be made from any attractive *jar, glass* or *bottle.* Using *white glue,* or other bonding preparation, paste on *dried split peas* in a close, uniform pattern directly on the glass. (See Figure 9-10A.) Some children might prefer to experiment with random designs. Allow time for drying. Spray with *white paint. Artificial flowers* or a *ribbon* may be added. (See Figure 9-10B.) Present to Mother, and be sure to attach your card!

Figure 9-10A

Figure 9-10B

Holland Tulip Time Festival

Holland Tulip Time Festival begins on the 14th of May. Festivals are conducted, and the Dutch cultural heritage is promoted.

A striking **tulip time bulletin board** can be made of *red* and *white*, or even *black* and *white 12" x 18" construction paper*.

Simply cut tulip(s) shapes from red paper and paste on white. Mount all pictures (move them around until an interesting, repetitive design composition is achieved) next to each other leaving no spaces between them. (See Figure 9-11A.)

Figure 9-11A

One or two bulletin boards can be filled in this way. Red, inch-wide strips can serve as a frame. The number of individual pictures needed depends on the size of the area to be covered.

Tulips can be cut wide or thin, large or small. One or more flowers may be used in each picture. Some tulips could be cut by folding the red paper like a fan to get several attached tulips at one time. (See Figure 9-11B.)

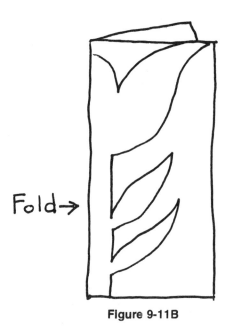

Fold→

Figure 9-11B

Buddha's Birthday

On May 18th, Buddha's Birthday, in Hong Kong, the statues of Lord Buddha are bathed, and observances of his birthday are held in the temples.

Many people wear jewelry fashioned in Buddha's image. Some charms are made of jade or other precious stones.

Clay figurines can be made in miniature form. Larger replicas can be modeled. Sprayed, or painted green or gold, they can become an interesting classroom display, leading to further exploration of Oriental gods.

Non-hardening clay might be preferable for use with younger children. If regular clay is used, be sure to hollow out the figure before kiln-firing.

Begin with a rectangular block of clay. Use wooden sticks and pencils to incise features and carve. A simple sketch, done before modeling, will enable children to see contours to be carved out more readily. Looking at different pictures of Buddha in various poses will help to keep this activity simple.

Some might prefer to approach the idea in another way. Attach a small clay ball for the head to a larger one for the body. Use "slip" (clay mixed with water) to attach. Pull out arms from the ball of clay, rather than sticking on extra pieces. Arms can be out-stretched, or close to body. (See Figures 9-12A and 9-12B.)

Figure 9-12A

Figure 9-12B

Add an imitation jewel to Buddha's navel!

If regular clay is used, experiment with colored glazes.

Another variation: Make Buddha from any bread dough recipe and wear as a pendant.

National Maritime Day

National Maritime Day (May 22) has been celebrated annually since 1933. President Franklin D. Roosevelt named this day in commemoration of the sailing of the steampowered ship *Savannah* which made the first steam crossing of the Atlantic, from Savannah, Georgia, to Liverpool, England, in 1819.

Children will enjoy making a simple **origami boat**, which requires the following of sequential directions. Boats can be made in different sizes, and put into pictures and box scenes.

Any *rectangular piece* of *paper* that folds easily will do. First, fold paper in half. Pinch top of folded edge to find the middle of the paper. Bring corners down to the middle until they meet. Fold up bottom edges on both sides until paper resembles a hat. Tuck in end flaps on both sides. Open up and press flat. Bring open bottom edge up to top on both sides. Open again, and press flat. Pull outward on top edges to form boat. Put finger in bottom to spread lightly, pinch top, and boat will stand. (See Figures 9-13A—9-13H.)

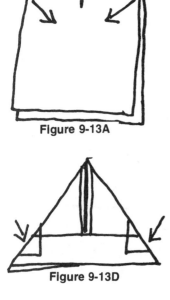

Figure 9-13A

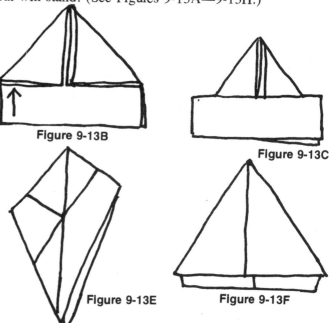

Figure 9-13B

Figure 9-13C

Figure 9-13D

Figure 9-13E

Figure 9-13F

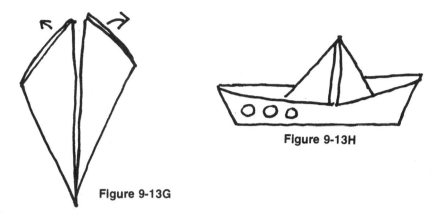

Figure 9-13H

Figure 9-13G

Decorate with portholes, mast and sails, if you wish. Make several, in different sizes and colors.

African Freedom Day

African Freedom Day, May 25, is celebrated unofficially here, and is a national holiday in Zambia. Contests, rallies and dances are sponsored by the members of the organization for African Unity.

The making of **African masks** can be stimulated by showing pictures and slides, easily obtainable from a school library or resource center.

Brown, strong paper (or a paper bag) is folded, and a simple, shield-like line, or even an oval, is drawn. Mouth and nose can be cut on the fold. Eyes and design-like shapes can be cut by poking the scissors through the double thickness. (See Figure 9-14A.) Open mask. Outline all open areas with *black marker* or *crayon* or *paint*, until mask is filled in completely with these interesting contour lines. Earrings of *paper* or *cardboard loops, feathers, ribbons, beads,* and *scrap fabric materials* will further enhance these creations.

Figure 9-14A

A paper band, stapled on, will enable the mask to be slipped over the head. Staple one end of band first, to ensure a proper fit. (See Figure 9-14B.)

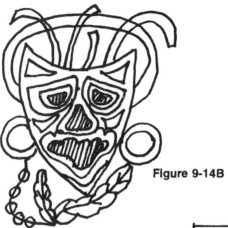

Figure 9-14B

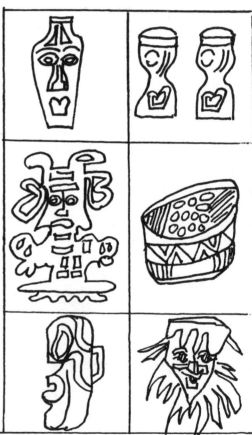

Figure 9-15

A second activity, **cloth patterns**, can introduce children to a simplified form of textile printing.

Use *same-size squares* of *unbleached muslin* or *sheeting,* and *wax crayons*. Create simple crayon patterns and/or figures, and iron carefully between pads of *newspaper*. Sew together to form a wall hanging. Leave edges free of design. (See Figure 9-15.) These can be washed. Use bright colors; press hard enough so wax will show through on other side when ironed.

Books and pictures on Africa and African motifs can be an inspiration. Many fascinating designs (sheets, towels, clothing) incorporating such ideas are on the market. Some children may own ''dashikis'' or other articles of African clothing.

Memorial Day

Memorial Day is a legal public holiday that falls on the last Monday in May. Sometimes called Decoration Day, it began to be observed in 1869, after the Civil War. People decorate the graves of soldiers with wreaths and flags on Decoration Day.

For this day of remembrance, children can hang up patriotic **three-dimensional spheres**.

Red, white, silver metallic, foil and *blue papers* can be transformed into spheres by a few scissor cuts.

Draw and cut a half circle from a folded paper rectangle. (See Figure 9-16A.) Lightweight paper 9″ x 12″ or 12″ x 18″ folds easily and stretches well. Do not open circle. Fold twice. Round off (trim edges), if not even. Paper should now resemble Figure 9-16B.

Make rounded cuts, always alternating sides. (See Figure 9-16C.)

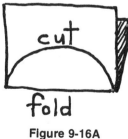

Figure 9-16A

Figure 9-16B   Figure 9-16C

Open carefully, so paper does not tear. Stretch down gently, grasping top. Tie the four open edges together with string to form sphere, which resembles a rounded, oval honeycomb.

Several spheres can be strung or clustered together. Shiny paper stars and stripes, or flowers, can be suspended from the center of the sphere by string. (See Figure 9-16D.)

Figure 9-16D

It is interesting to children to discover that the original paper circle has expanded so far behind its original shape.

A second appropriate Memorial Day project would be a large **parade mural**. It can be executed on any size *roll* of *paper* and cut to size desired. Tack to wall or bulletin board, or lay on the floor. Children can sketch figures directly, or cut from *newspaper*, pin the best ones onto the paper, trace and remove. If done by the latter method, the figures can be lifted and repeated elsewhere on the mural. Group some figures, let others "march" alone. *Paint* or *color*, hang up and enjoy the marching spirit! (See Figure 9-17.)

Festival of Weeks (Shabuoth)

Festival of Weeks (Shabuoth) is a Jewish holy day celebrating the onset of the spring grain harvest. Children of all religions can benefit from the creation of **grain and seed pictures**.

Supermarkets yield *rice* (pearled and plain), *barley, lentils, peas, beans* (red, kidney, navy and blackeye), *sunflower seeds*, etc. *Kitchen spices* may also be employed in your design. Sketch a

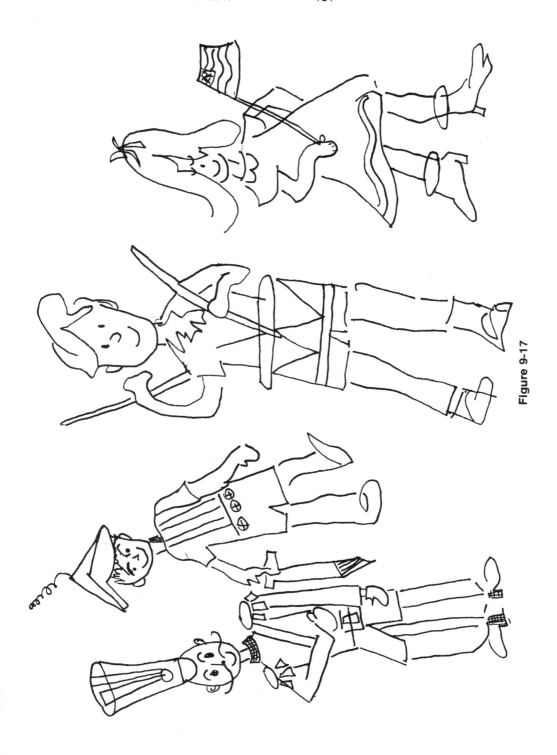

Figure 9-17

nature-inspired or abstract picture on *heavy paper* or a *piece* of *scrap board*. Keep seeds separated. *Plastic trays* with compartments are ideal for this purpose. Using a *white glue*, set in seeds, and continue until the composition is completed. Keep in mind textures and colors and their juxtaposition. (See Figure 9-18.)

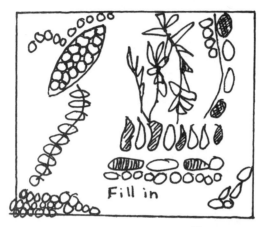

Figure 9-18

Edges of board can be framed with *colored* or *black heavy tape*. Add a *hook* for hanging, and your plaque can become an attractive addition to any kitchen decor.

A **straw scarecrow** certainly lends itself to harvest activities. *Weeds, corn husks,* or *excelsior* may be used.

Creating your straw man is fun. All types of *scrap fabric*, even a man's old *hat*, can be brought from home. The scarecrow can be

Figure 9-19

mounted on *wood* or *heavy paper* for a bulletin board display, or stuffed with rags and propped up in a chair. Use your imagination!

The head can be cloth wrapped around a *newspaper* core, with *button* eyes. *Vegetables* like *carrots* and *peppers* become ears or a nose. *Straw* can be wrapped around *twigs* for arms and legs. Real *shoes* or *sneakers* can be an amusing addition. (See Figure 9-19.)

Bonus Activities for May

Birthday of First Postage Stamp

May 6th commemorates the birthday of the first postage stamp (penny black of Great Britain). On May 6, 1840, the first stamp was issued. Many children become interested in philately at an early age.

To create **miniature stamps,** *gummed paper tape* in different colors can be used. Look at several stamps and discuss for motivation. Words and stamp monetary values can be added, using *other types* of *papers* and *fine-line markers*. Use on regular or class-designed envelopes, make a class mailbox, and send surprise letters to classmates. (See Figure 9-20.)

Figure 9-20

Captain Kidd Tried for Piracy

On the 9th of May, in 1701, Captain Kidd was tried for piracy.

All children are excited by the idea of pirates and treasure hunts!

To make **pirate hats**, use *stiff 15" x 18" paper* and fold in half. Pinch to find middle of fold. Bring down top corners until they meet. Top will be pointed. Fold up bottom edges on both sides. Staple together. Add loops of stiff paper for pirate earrings. (See Figures 9-21A—9-21C.)

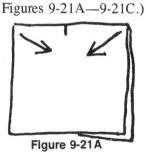

Figure 9-21A

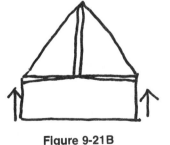

Figure 9-21B

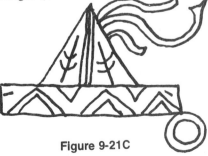

Figure 9-21C

Decorate as you please. Curl strips for streamers. Draw a buried treasure map, and set up a classroom hunt!

Ben Franklin Invents Bifocals

Benjamin Franklin announced his invention of bifocal eyeglasses on May 23, 1785. Children of all ages enjoy playing with **make-believe glasses.**

Fold *heavy black construction paper* in half. Draw as indicated in Figure 9-22.

Paste *yellow cellophane* or *light colored tissue paper* on back of cut-out eye hole areas and trim. Have fun—but do not wear these ''glasses'' outside if you cannot see clearly!

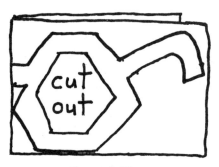

Figure 9-22

Indians Sell Manhattan to Peter Minuit

On May 24, 1626, the Indians sold Manhattan Island to Peter Minuit for $24 worth of trinkets.

Trinket jewelry can be made from seeds, safety pins, pop-tops, modeling clay and clay recipes, macaroni, beads, etc. All that is necessary is *string* (elasticized works well), wool, a *needle* for punching and stringing and ingenuity.

One favorite is a **paper clip necklace**. Materials needed: *contact paper* in any color and *72 paper clips* for each necklace.

Directions: Cut contact paper strips into one-inch strips. Peel away the backing slightly. Center paper clip ¼ inch from the top, and fold paper down over it. Cut ¼ inch below the clip. Fold up and

press tightly, to prevent popping open. Put two covered clips together. Insert uncovered clip through both, and cover. Repeat. Keep
seams inside. (See Figure 9-23.) Wear proudly, or give as a gift!

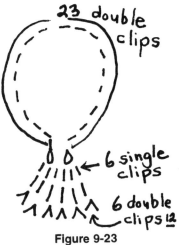

Figure 9-23

10

HIGHLIGHTS

 ### of the month of

JUNE

America the Beautiful Week

First Successful Ford Automobile

Frank Lloyd Wright's Birthday

Comstock Lode Discovered

Henry David Thoreau's Birthday

Flag Day

Father's Day

Summer Begins

Vacation Begins

Commencement Day

Telegraph Service Inaugurated (New York—Boston)

Freedom Week

America the Beautiful Week

We celebrate America the Beautiful Week June 1 through 7. The purpose is to enjoy and encourage the preservation of our natural resources. In many places, people have made America more beautiful by planting trees, creating gardens, and keeping certain areas free from commercial interference.

Using *oaktag* (or paper similar in stiffness) cut to postcard size, *water colors* and *small brushes*, children can make their own delicate **scenic cards** and mail to friends and family.

Commercial postcards, notepapers, photographs and reproductions of paintings can be studied for motivation prior to this activity. A trip to a local park or other unspoiled area might be initiated for on-the-spot sketching. Leaves, ferns, flowers and stones should be examined for possible enlargement, with attention to detail.

Scale should be discussed, as the actual working space will be small.

Perhaps several pencil sketches can be done, and the most successful used for the final postcard painting.

A dry brush technique, where a minimum of water is used, might be one approach.

Another could be a wet-in-wet handling of the medium, where colors are tipped into the paper, which is first wet heavily with water. Colors will flow and blend into each other, creating an interesting background for ink or dry brush detail.

A follow-up lesson could be evaluation and discussion of the elements of the most successful efforts.

For one example, see Figure 10-1.

Figure 10-1

First Successful Ford Automobile

On the 4th of June, the first successful automobile was driven by Henry Ford in Detroit. The year was 1896, the start of America's intense preoccupation with the car.

Most children are both familiar and comfortable with this important means of transportation. Many will choose the automobile image over and over again in their drawings.

One activity, **double-image pictures**, requires *two issues* of the *same magazine*. Colored pictures of cars may be preferable to black and white, but experimentation with both can be interesting.

Remove the same two pictures selected from both magazines. Cut horizontal strips straight across each page, about an inch wide. Vertical cutting can be tried at another time. Strips may be cut on the paper cutter.

Take special care to keep the strips in proper order.

On a *sheet* of *construction paper* (12″ x 18″) paste the first strip from one page, then the first from the second page, thus repeating, or elongating, the image. Do not leave a space between them.

You may need to attach a second sheet of construction paper, if you choose to use the entire magazine page, but this is not necessary to produce the desired effect. (See Figure 10-2.)

Figure 10-2

Double image pictures will be quite fascinating. When all are mounted and displayed on the bulletin board or in the hall, everyone will wonder just how they were done.

As a variation, try pictures of close-up faces for yet another interesting result.

Frank Lloyd Wright's Birthday

Frank Lloyd Wright, famous American architect, was born June 8, 1867, in Richland Center, Wisconsin. He died on April 9, 1959, in Phoenix, Arizona. This great pioneer is considered the lawgiver of modern architecture. His genius for structure culminated in the construction of the Guggenheim Museum in New York City, when he was almost ninety years old.

Elementary school children can experiment with simple building forms made of paper.

An easy technique, requiring *scissors, construction paper* and *tape* (or a stapler), is called **lock and tab**.

Cut a wide strip to begin. At one end, cut a tab shape. Cut a slit (by poking scissors) in the middle of the other end, and join. (See Figure 10-3A.) If younger children have difficulty with this procedure, the tab can be taped on the inside.

Shapes should vary in size and width; some should be horizontal and some vertical.

Windows and doors can be cut by folding the strip(s) at intervals, before inserting the tab into the slit.

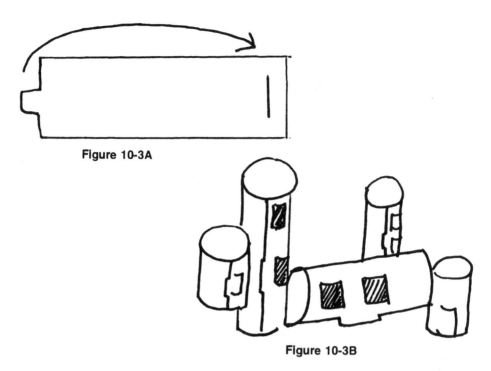

Figure 10-3A

Figure 10-3B

Several forms, when completed, can be joined with tape or staples to create building "units" suitable for decoration in any media—markers to paint. (See Figure 10-3B.)

Comstock Lode Discovered

The Comstock Lode, a silver mine in Nevada, was discovered on June 11 in 1859.

Silver remains a precious metal, and is utilized in many ways besides as legal tender.

Children are familiar with play money from the profusion of games on the market.

Technically, today's "silver" coins are a combination of alloys, like copper, but they can certainly serve in this project. Dimes, nickels, quarters, half dollars and silver dollars can be "reproduced" quite easily by rubbing with a pencil.

Many youngsters have already tried **coin rubbing** at home and in school, but if both front and back sides of *coin* are rubbed, they can be cut out and pasted to same size *cardboard circles* with *white glue*, and used for math practice and play.

Place the coin under the paper. Use a bond or other soft paper, and hold securely, until impression appears. Rub with the side of the pencil lead. Coin rubbings can also be done with *crayon*.

Henry David Thoreau's Birthday

Henry David Thoreau, New England author best known for *Walden*, was born in 1817 and died in 1862. The birthday of this nature lover and writer is celebrated on June 12th.

Discuss and show examples of impressionistic art, such as the work of Vincent Van Gogh. A simple explanation or introduction to the technique of **pointillism** would be valuable. Pointillism is the optical phenomenon by which dots of pure, precise, complementary colors, seen at a distance, tend to blend into new, mixed colors in the human eye. It became the basis for the artist Seurat's pointillist brush techniques.

Children might first attempt small pictures on *paper* made solely with dots of color, applied by *crayon* or *paint*, to see the resulting effect. Several small pictures can be mounted together.

If nature is used as the theme, some charming results will be obtained through practice.

Flag Day

Flag Day is June 14th of each year by Presidential proclamation. It is the anniversary of the creation of the first red, white and blue national banner, which was accepted in 1777 by the Continental Congress.

The red signified daring, the white, purity, and the blue stood for anti-oppression, incorporating vigilance, justice and perseverance.

The first American flag to fly over a school was at Catamount Hills, Massachusetts, in 1812.

For a large **bulletin board flag**, thirteen *red* and *white* alternating stripes of *paper* are cut. They can be wavy or straight. Loops of rolled paper can be tried, also.

On a blue paper field, carefully staple thirteen 3-D stars so they remain dimensional.

Cutting the star(s) involves a few simple steps. Practice cutting several sizes, and save extra stars for other projects.

Begin with a rectangular piece of white paper, 6″ x 9″ or 9″ x 12″. Fold in half, the short way. Keep the fold at the top. Bring the upper left corner over and down to the middle of the right hand side of the folded paper. Press and crease. Fold right corner triangle over and down, to meet fold formed. Fold left side over right to form a triangle. Paper now resembles an upside-down cone shape. Take small triangle out and fold over. Cut on a sharp diagonal, following diagram. Open.

Upper part is a five-pointed star. Re-crease the folds of the star in and out (*up* on points; *down* on connecting areas) to get the dimensional effect. (See Figures 10-4A—10-4E.)

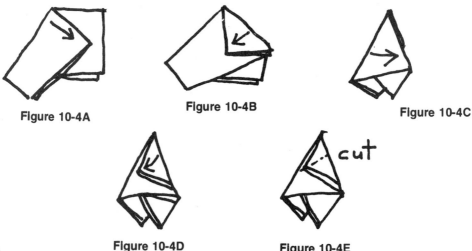

Figure 10-4A

Figure 10-4B

Figure 10-4C

Figure 10-4D

Figure 10-4E

Figure 10-5A

Figure 10-5B

Paper loop hangings, festive and patriotic in appearance, look best when hung at intervals with string from classroom lighting fixtures.

Red, white and *blue one-inch strips* of *12″ x 18″ construction paper* and a *hand stapler* are all the materials needed.

Begin with three 18″ long, one-inch strips, one of each color.

Staple them together, according to diagram (Figure 10-5A). Continue adding strips, filling in loops with circles, swirls, zig-zag pieces, etc. Symmetrical or asymmetrical balance can be achieved. Some strips may be cut in half, some edges may be curled or fringed, according to whim.

Continue adding strips and loops until desired length is obtained. Pupil results will vary.

Punch a hole in the top, add a string, and suspend (Figure 10-5B).

Father's Day

Father's Day is the third Sunday in June. The first official celebration was on June 19, 1910. Mrs. John Bruce Dodd, the Ministerial Association, and the Y.M.C.A. of Washington were the sponsors.

Children can include brothers, uncles, and grandfathers when cards and gifts are made.

For an original **necktie card**, a large paper tie bearing dad's name can be made and worn for fun.

Draw, on the fold of a 12″ x 18″ piece of *white construction paper*, half of a large, simple tie shape. (See Figure 10-6A.)

Cut out and open. Turn sideways. Write (cursive only) dad's first name on the fold with a pencil. Re-fold paper, and rub hard on the back of tie to transfer the name to other side. Open. Go over the lines to preserve them. Color in some sections to create an interesting design. Name can still be read if tie is held sideways. (See Figure 10-6B.) This is basically the same procedure used in the September lesson called "Pencil Rubbings."

Figure 10-6A

Figure 10-6B

Shirt and tie card seems to be a favorite with children. It can be made in different sizes, from 3″ x 8″ (folded in half) to 12″ x 18″ (unfolded).

If card is folded, a greeting can be written on the inside.

Cut in on both sides from folded edge (top of card), and staple to form the shirt collar. (See Figure 10-7A.) Cut a paper tie (don't forget the knot) and staple under the collar. Tie and collar can be connected with one staple, which serves as a tie pin.

Cut (or draw) pockets, a handkerchief, stripes, etc., to complete the shirt front.

A cut paper "price tag" can be attached with a string. (See Figure 10-7B.)

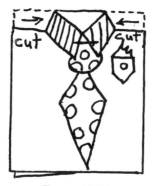

Figure 10-7A

Figure 10-7B

For a **pop-up card**, a funny face on a spring produces a surprising effect.

Fold *any color paper* suitable for a greeting card in half. On the front, letter with *crayon* or *ink*: ''Just *Pop*ping Up to Say'' . . .On the inside, write ''Have a Happy Father's Day!''

Make a short spring of *two small strips* of paper, folded at right angles, or simply one strip bent back and forth. Attach a humorous face with glue or tape so spring is not visible. Paste other end of spring to the inside of the card. (See Figures 10-8A and 10-B.)

Using the pop-up theme, encourage children to make up other, original greetings.

Figure 10-8A

Figure 10-8B

Summer Begins

Summer begins on the 21st or 22nd of June, when the sun appears at its highest point.

When the weather turns warm, and plans for vacation are beginning, children can make a **movable happy face**, in anticipation.

On a large piece of white construction paper, about 12″ x 18″, draw the head of a boy or girl.

Color the hair and draw in the nose. Make two vertical slits at sides of the face where the eyes would be. Do the same for the mouth area. (See Figure 10-9A.) Cut two long strips of white paper, about one or two inches wide. On one strip, draw as many different pairs of eyes as will fit. Leave a small space between each pair. On the other strip, draw several kinds of mouths.

Insert strips into slits on the head. Pull through, slowly, to change expression. (See Figure 10-9B.)

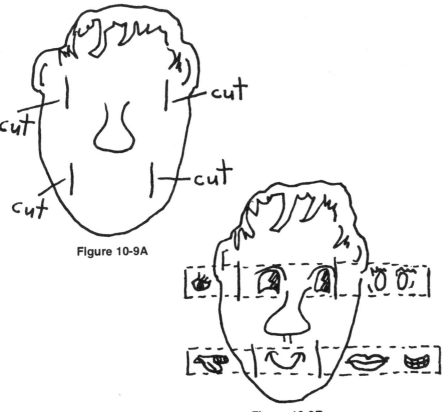

Figure 10-9A

Figure 10-9B

Strips may be fastened with paste or tape in back of the face to form a continuous loop.

Use a sneaker for a model and introduce **detailed object line drawing** to your class.

White paper and pencil (or markers) are needed.

Place the sneaker where all see it. Children will be viewing it from different angles.

Discuss details: laces, worn spots, stitching, etc. (See Figures 10-10A and 10-10B.)

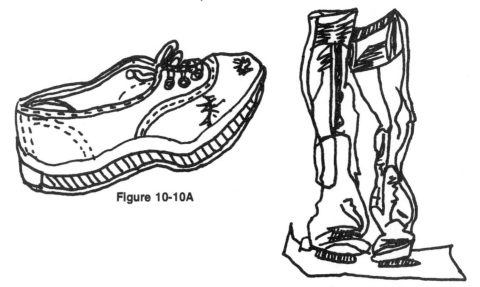

Figure 10-10A

Figure 10-10B

Variations on this lesson can include coloring or painting the sneaker for added realism; using two sneakers as in a still-life arrangement; using shoes or boots instead of sneakers.

For additional lessons, a contour approach may be tried. Look only at the sneaker, not at the paper. Do not lift the pencil from the paper. Draw the sneaker in one continuous line.

Exaggeration for effect is another way to approach this activity. Larger than actual size, or "blow-up," will be the result.

Students will be surprised and delighted at the degree of accuracy and realism they can obtain after a few attempts.

Display and enjoy!

Several primary teachers I know have framed their **memory collages**.

Children draw themselves, color and cut out the figures. Then they place them on poster board or similar sturdy paper, overlapping some figures, until a pleasing arrangement is achieved. All the children should join in this decision-making process. (See Figure 10-11.)

Figure 10-11

White glue is preferable to paper paste.

Sizes of the figures will vary, adding to the interest of the composition.

Names can be added to the collage, along with the date and name of school.

What teacher wouldn't be pleased with this special remembrance of her class?

Vacation Begins

Some activities for summer fun can be started in June.

A paper **checkerboard game** is fun to make and enjoyable to play with. Since most children have had some experience in weaving paper strips, all that is necessary is a careful count to reproduce a real checkerboard. Eight strips of *black paper*, about one inch wide, create alternating squares of four red and four black, when *red paper* is used for the "loom." (See Figures 10-12A and 10-12B.)

Even if weaving produces the wrong count, crop the paper to the proper number of squares and mount on *cardboard*.

Checkerboard playing area will be about 8″ x 9″, but 9″ x 12″ paper may be used. The excess becomes a border. Paper circles (checkers) of red and black can be cut and pasted on cardboard for strength. Checkers can be kept in a small envelope of folded paper created for this purpose, or in a small box.

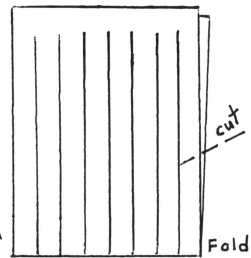

Figure 10-12A

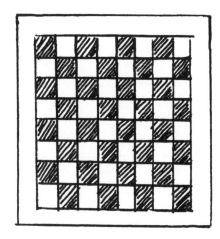

Figure 10-12B

Color wheels that spin, showing primary colors changing to secondary, are created easily by following the diagram in Figure 10-13.

Trace a circle and cut out. Try different sizes.

Younger children might find it easier to follow these lines on a dittoed sheet, which can be colored and pasted on cardboard.

Be sure to stress heavy coloring for best results.

Poke a hole with a *straight pin* or nail in the center of the circle. Hold pin and spin fast.

Red and blue blend and become purple; yellow and blue merge to green; red and yellow turn orange.

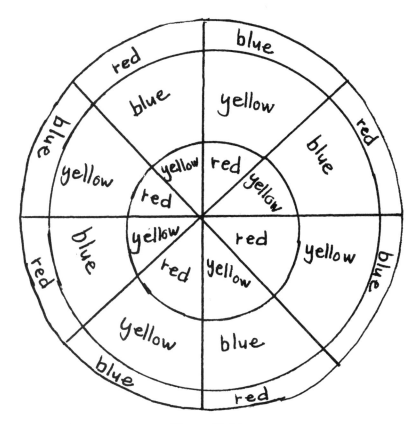

Figure 10-13

What a simple way to get this concept across!

A **wearable art activity** is quite a conversation piece!

Materials needed: box of *animal cookies, pin backs* (obtainable at craft stores), *clear nail polish,* and *clear liquid glue*.

Figure 10-14

Affix pin back (in open position) at back of cookie with clear glue. Let dry. (See Figure 10-14.) Apply two or three coats of clear nail polish, front and back, sealing the whole cookie. Let dry, between coats, on waxed paper.

For variations of the same idea, try pearlized nail polish, or paint dots and designs on cookie with acrylic paints. Then spray with a fixative or varnish.

These pins are fun to wear and will produce compliments.

Use baker's clay or bread dough recipes to create original animal pins from scratch.

Bonus Activities

Commencement Day

Some children might have older brothers and sisters who are nearing the day they will graduate from high school or college—Commencement Day.

To celebrate this happy time, **party favors** can be made. *White* and *black paper*, along with some *string* and *ribbon*, are needed.

For a diploma, roll a 6″ x 5″ (approximate size) piece of stiff white paper into a tight cylinder. The edges can be cut so they are somewhat concave. Add a fancy ribbon or wool bow, tied in the middle. The graduate's name, date of graduation and school can be inscribed in ink in fancy writing for a nostalgic keepsake. (See Figure 10-15A.)

Figure 10-15A

For the graduation cap, a 4″ x 5″ rectangle of *black* or *white paper* is used for the brim, and a 3″ x 6″ piece, folded into quarters and stapled, is inserted into it. Cut out a diamond-shaped piece from the brim before insertion.

Cover the top of the cap with a white paper insert, and paste on a real, covered button, or one made of paper. If paper is used, cut several small circles and paste together for thickness. or use black heavy poster or mat board.

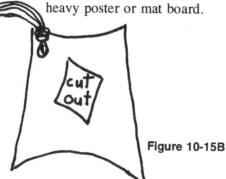

cut out

Figure 10-15B

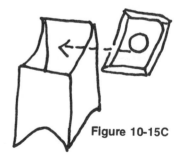

Figure 10-15C

Half of the cap will be above the brim, and half below. Cut edges on part below so they are concave. Attach a string tassel to one edge of the brim. (See Figures 10-15B–10-15C.)

Put one of each next to every plate at the party.

Telegraph Service Inaugurated (New York—Boston)

On the 27th of June, in 1847, telegraph service was inaugurated between New York City and Boston.

Original telegraph signals were probably as incomprehensible to Americans as ancient Egyptian hieroglyphics. Defined as a picture or symbol representing a word, syllable or sound, hieroglyphics were used instead of alphabet letters.

Direct the children in cutting several *white* squares one or one and one-half inches in size. The aim is to cut each square so that it is altered, and different from all the others. Do not allow any predrawing. The square may be folded before cutting. Edges can be cut into or cut off.

The most interesting squares are then selected and arranged on a *black* background in crossword puzzle fashion. Result: **American hieroglyphics**! (See Figure 10-16.)

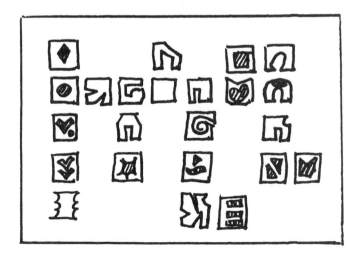

Figure 10-16

Children can make up meanings for their symbols and compose original stories, thus incorporating language arts into this activity.

A second lesson requires a pile of *newspapers*, some *yellow paper*, *scissors* and *paste*. Children hunt for letters and phrases to create their own telegrams. They can decide to limit it to ten words or compose longer messages. These telegrams can be "delivered" to classmates or read aloud.

Freedom Week

June 27 through July 4 is designated as Freedom Week. Attention is focused on America's heritage.

July 4th, or Independence Day, is celebrated in many ways. Any party-goer will enjoy **firecracker favors**.

Wrap short cardboard paper tubes in brightly colored *crepe* or *tissue paper*. Longer tubes (from inside paper towels) may be cut down to size.

Alternating stripes of red, white and blue would be most appropriate. Cut and fringe the edges. Fill with *hard candy* or other treats before twisting the ends tightly. (See Figure 10-17.)

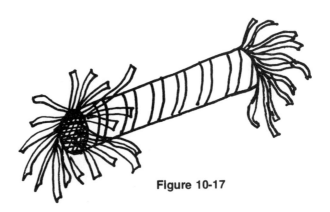

Figure 10-17

Index